# WORLD CUP CRICKET

First published in 2019
by Murray Books (Australia)
www.murraybooks.com
This edition published in 2019

ISBN: 9781782814917

Authors : Rajesh Kumar & Kersi Meher-Homji
Compiled by Peter Murray

Images: Shutterstock, Getty Images

# CONTENTS

# CRICKET WORLD CUP

## PETER MURRAY

Peter has four decades of cricket writing and publishing behind him. Born in India, he migrated to Australia in 1967. Since attending the 1983 World Cup in England when he travelled with the India team, he has produced books for several World Cup's alongside Rajesh Kumar. He has had several best-selling books including *Chappell, Lillee Marsh, Tendulkar Masterful* and *Cricket World Cup 1983*.

## RAJESH KUMAR

Apart from a regular contributor in the cricketing bible, *Wisden Cricketers' Almanack* and *The Times of India* for over three decades, Rajesh has brought out five World Cup editions for Australia's leading publisher, Peter Murray. Assisted Bill Frindall, the doyen of cricket statisticians since 1980 till his death in January 2009 during the publications of *The Wisden Book of Test Cricket, The Guinness Book of Cricket Facts and Feats, The Wisden Book of Cricket Records, Limited-Overs International Cricket* and *Playfair Cricket Annual*.

## KERSI MEHER-HOMJI

Kersi is an author of 15 cricket books including *The Waugh Twins, Cricket's Great All-rounders, Six Appeal* and *Nervous Nineties*. He writes regularly for *Inside Cricket, Roar, The Indian Down Under* and other publications. He has recently published his new book on *From Bradman to Kohli* - Best of Australia - India Test cricket with Forewords by Allan Border and Sunil Gavaskar.

# CRICKET WORLD CUP
## 1975 ENGLAND

### RAJESH KUMAR

## West Indies - the first one-day World Cup Champions

Forty eight years ago, on January 5, 1971, cricket history was created when Australia and England met in the first 'official' Limited-Overs International at the Melbourne Cricket Ground, arranged hastily on the scheduled last day to compensate the public of Victoria after unseasonal rain had ruined the third Test, and was abandoned without a ball being bowled.

It was a well-attended game, attracting 46,006 match-starved Melbournians desperate for some cricket. The innovation was an immediate success. Since then, Limited-Overs Internationals have become the most popular brand of cricket.

The outstanding success of the first ever One Day International compelled the authorities in England to commence single-innings limited-overs internationals on a series basis. During the Australian team's visit to England in 1972, instead of a sixth Test, the Prudential Trophy came into existence, when three 55-over matches between England and the visiting Australians were contested at Old Trafford, Lord's and Edgbaston. England won that Prudential Trophy series by two matches to one. In financial terms, the tournament attracted gate receipts of £46,000.

The format of one-day internationals became so popular in England that it was eagerly copied in other cricket-playing countries. It had everything that cricket lovers wanted - lots of action, runs, wickets, run-outs, sixes and a guaranteed result within the space of a day.

Because of the immense popularity of limited-overs one-day internationals, the Prudential World Cup, 60-over a side, finally took place in June 1975 in England, an ideal venue with plenty of adequate grounds and with not too much travelling required. Blessed with perfect weather during the entire fortnight and enjoyed by large audiences, it produced receipts of over £88,598.

The six Tests' playing nations, England, West Indies, India, Australia, Pakistan and New Zealand were joined by two associate members, Sri Lanka and East Africa to make up a total of eight competitors, initially playing round-robin matches in two groups of four, with the top two in each group going into a knock-out semi-final.

England topped Group A, recording cakewalk victories against India, New Zealand and East Africa with some ease. New Zealand secured second place. In Group B, the stronger group, West Indies also won all three matches but after an extraordinary nail-biting finish to their match against Pakistan at Birmingham. In response to Pakistan's healthy total of 266 for seven wickets, West Indies regularly lost wickets and were 203 for nine at one stage but thanks to an undefeated last-wicket

# CRICKET WORLD CUP
## 1975 ENGLAND

### RAJESH KUMAR

partnership of 64 between wicketkeeper Deryck Murray (61 not out) and Andy Roberts (24 not out), snatched an epic victory with two balls to spare. Australia qualified for the semi-finals as runners-up, thanks to victories over Pakistan and Sri Lanka.

The two semi-finals between West Indies & New Zealand and England & Australia were exciting cricket nonetheless. Headingley, Leeds was the venue of the semi-final tie between the two arch-rivals, England and Australia. The strip was uneven and the ball kept low - the game lasted just 65 overs. Put into bat, the Englishmen were reeling at 36 for six at the end of the 18th over, with left-arm swing bowler, Gary Gilmour, taking full advantage of the conditions, claiming all six wickets at a cost of just ten runs. His final bowling analysis of 12-6-14-6 remained the record until the 1983 World Cup when West Indies' Winston Davis captured 7 wickets for 51 runs at the same ground.

England were dismissed for just 93 runs off 36.2 overs and only their captain, Mike Denness (27) and Geoff Arnold (18 not out), who came out to bat at number ten, reached double figures. Understandably, Australia, in response, batted cautiously but the run-scoring was not easier and lost six wickets in accomplishing the target, Gilmour (28 not out) coming to the rescue with the bat. With Doug Walters (20 not out), he shared an unbroken winning partnership of 55 after Australia had been reduced to 39 for six by Geoff Arnold (1/15), John Snow (2/30) and Chris Old (3/29). With his excellent all-round performance - best bowling analysis and highest individual score in the match - Gilmour (right) won the day for Australia. He was deservingly named the Man of the Match - his second and last MOM award in ODIs.

New Zealand, put in by Clive Lloyd in the other semi-final at The Oval, could manage just 158 in 52.2 overs. After John Morrison's dismissal at 8, an outstanding slip catch by Rohan Kanhai off Andy Roberts ended captain's Glenn Turner's innings, who had scored 36, but before his departure, he had put on 90 runs off 141 balls with Geoff Howarth (51) for the second wicket. However, the remaining eight batsmen only added 60 runs. The inability of the New Zealand middle-order batsmen to capitalise on the solid start, denied the spectators the chance of witnessing an absorbing encounter. The West Indian fast bowlers - Bernard Julien (4 for 27), Vanburn Holder (3 for 30) and Andy Roberts (2 for 18) - bowled splendidly and were in complete control of the situation throughout.

In response, the West Indians, who were just 159 runs away from a place in the first ever World Cup Final, achieved their target with almost twenty overs to spare, winning by five wickets. Gordon Greenidge (55) and Alvin Kallicharran (72) with their 125-run stand for the second wicket, ensured a comfortable victory for their side. For

# CRICKET WORLD CUP
## 1975 ENGLAND

New Zealand, the aggressive and accurate display of left-arm fast bowling by Richard Collinge (3 for 28) was some consolation. Kallicharran was justifiably adjudged the Man of the Match.

The aforesaid 125-run partnership remains the only second-wicket stand for the West Indies in the semi-finals/finals in World Cup.

Glenn Turner, with 333 runs (ave.166.50), including two hundreds, in four innings, top-scored in the competition. He remained the only batsman to manage 300 runs apart from hitting two centuries (171 not out vs East Africa at Birmingham on June 7 and 114 not out vs India at Manchester on June 14) and maintain an average of 150-plus. Among the captains with 300 runs or more in the World Cup, his average is the highest.

The final of the first ever World Cup was contested between the two best teams of the tournament on the longest day of the year - 21st June. The match provided cricket of the highest quality, with millions watching on television from 11 am until 8.42 pm.

Put into bat, the West Indians had been reduced to 50 for three in the 18th over but their captain Clive Lloyd (right) batted brilliantly to post an 82-ball hundred. He was associated in a partnership of 149 in 26 overs with Rohan Kanhai (55 off 105 balls) for the fourth wicket - the highest by any fourth-wicket pair in the final of the World Cup apart from the highest for any wicket-position for the West Indies as well as by any pair against Australia in the final of the World Cup.

Thanks to their century partnership, followed by a 52-run stand from ten overs for the seventh wicket between Keith Boyce (34) and Bernard Julien (26 not out), West Indies registered 291 for eight in their allotted 60 overs. The said stand remains the only fifty-plus partnership for the seventh wicket in the final of the World Cup.

Gary Gilmour performed admirably to bag five wickets conceding 48 runs - his victims being Kallicharran, Kanhai, Lloyd, Richards and Murray. He remains the only bowler to produce a five-wicket haul each in the semi-final and the final of the same tournament. His tally of eleven wickets in just two matches, remained a record for the inaugural World Cup. His bowling average (5.63) strike rate (13.0) and economy rate (2.58) were outstanding.

# CRICKET WORLD CUP
## 1975 ENGLAND

### RAJESH KUMAR

Undaunted by their immense task, Australia fought to the very end and might well have achieved a remarkable win if half their wickets had not fallen to run outs - three key batsmen (opener Alan Turner, Greg Chappell and Ian Chappell) by Viv Richards - including direct hits from mid-wicket and cover. Steven Lynch had remarked in his piece, namely, Richards runs out three in Cricinfo in 2009: "In those days giving the Man of the Match award to a fielder would have been a bit too adventurous, and Lloyd got it for his terrific ton. But it was Richards who won that first final."

The Australian captain, Ian Chappell was a picture of confidence from the word go, making 62 off 93 balls. At one stage, they were 221 for six and appeared to be in the hunt until Keith Boyce (4 for 50) and a string of run outs caused their downfall. Australia's ninth wicket fell at 233 but a defiant last-wicket partnership of 41 between Jeff Thomson (21 off 21 balls) and Dennis Lillee (16 not out off 19 balls) took Australia within range of their target before Thomson, sent back when attempting a bye to the wicketkeeper, was beaten by Murray's underarm throw and the West Indies, with a 17-run triumph, had won the World Cup. Australia were all out for 274 off 58.4 overs.

Clive Lloyd (right), the man of the match, received the Prudential Cup from the Duke of Edinburgh as the West Indies were crowned the first one-day World Champions. The West Indian skipper later admitted this was his greatest moment in cricket.

The tournament earnings exceeded £200,000 - the total attendance for the 15 games was 158,000. The attendance in the final at Lord's was 26,000. The winners, West Indies received £4,000, runners-up, Australia received £2,000 while the losing semi-finalists, New Zealand and England each received £1,000. The Test and County Cricket Board (TCCB) received 10% of the profits as hosts and the other seven participating teams each received 7%.

The exhilarating cricket, consisting of just 15 World Cup matches on only five playing days during the 15-day span, was a resounding success and the first World Cup made the sport even more popular not only in England but all over the cricketing World. With this, Limited-Overs Internationals finally came of age.

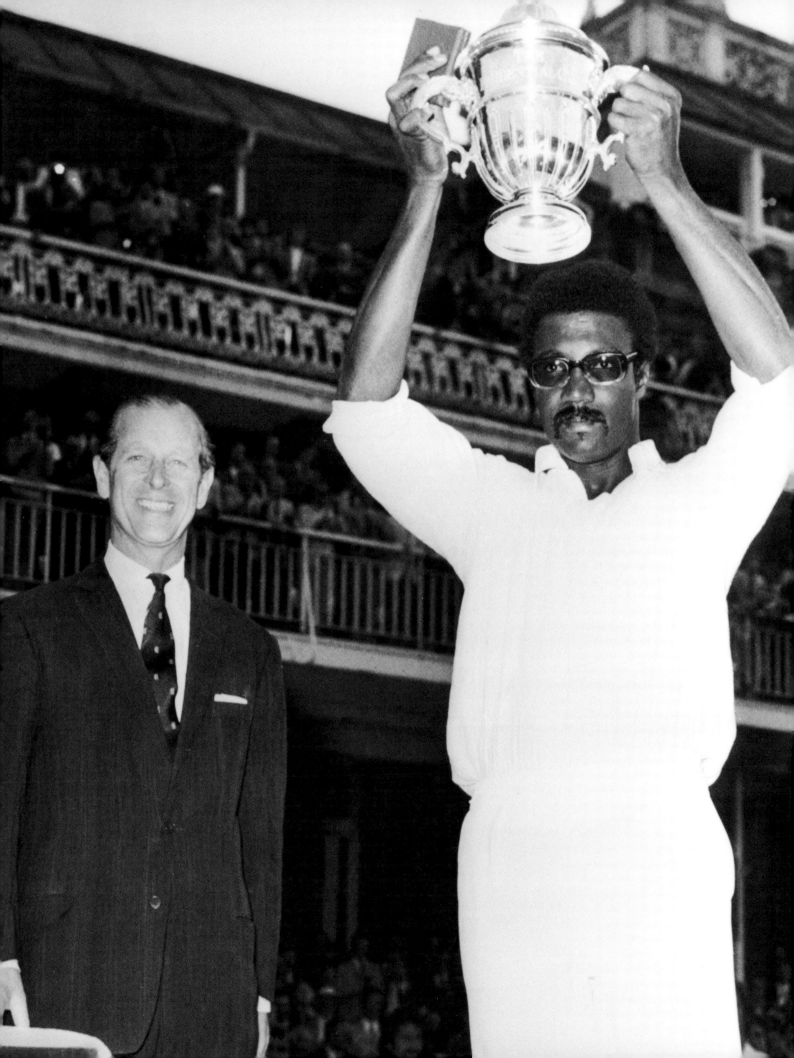

# CRICKET WORLD CUP
# 1979 ENGLAND

## RAJESH KUMAR

## The Windies win again

Despite the introduction of international limited-overs cricket as a permanent feature of the English summer, the Australian authorities stubbornly refused to change their attitude towards instant cricket. It was only after the grand success of Kerry Packer's World Series Cricket in 1977-78 (which gave the game a new, exciting image in Australia and in other cricket-playing countries and revolutionized crowd involvement) that the Australian Cricket Board bowed to the inevitable and staged a three-match series against England in 1978-79.

The second Prudential World Cup, contested in England in 1979, proved to be another outstanding success overall. Despite the drop in attendances, caused by poor weather, increased prices meant that gate receipts amounted to £359,700 while profits amounted to £350,000. The West Indies, confirming their prowess as an outstanding team, again won the final.

The competition was run on a similar format and time frame to its predecessor, constituting a schedule of 15 matches, contested between eight teams. As in the previous tournament, the teams participating in the Prudential World Cup were divided into two groups of four, each playing the other once but this time, England and Australia were not seeded. The top two nations in each group would then contest the semi finals, followed by a final at Lord's. South Africa was not considered again.

Group A comprised England, Pakistan, Australia and Canada while Group B consisted of the West Indies, New Zealand, Sri Lanka and India. England topped their Group with three victories - vs Australia by six wickets; vs Canada by eight wickets and vs Pakistan by 14 runs. Pakistan finished runners-up, thanks to a vital triumph over the previous beaten finalists, Australia by 89 runs. West Indies, who were hot favourites to retain the title, topped the table in Group B easily. New Zealand secured the runners-up spot, beating Sri Lanka by 9 wickets and India by 8 wickets.

Sri Lanka's surprise win over India by 47 runs at Old Trafford, their first World Cup victory, was the major highlight in the group stage.

In the semi-final, England, in front of an almost capacity crowd of 22,000 sneaked home against New Zealand at Old Trafford by just 9 runs, which was at that time the narrowest margin of victory in a World Cup encounter. After being put into bat by Mark Burgess, England's batting failed to come to terms with the steady bowling. Thanks to Graham Gooch (71), skipper Mike Brearley (53) and Derek Randall (42 not out), they could manage 221 runs for eight wickets, which meant that the target for New Zealand was well under four runs per over.

# CRICKET WORLD CUP
## 1979 ENGLAND

### RAJESH KUMAR

In a fluctuating game, at 180 for six, the New Zealanders were in the hunt but then Warren Lees and Lance Cairns both fell to Mike Hendrick. Their last pair Brian McKechnie and Gary Troup required 14 runs off the final over from Ian Botham but they finished on 212 for nine with John Wright scoring 69 off 137 balls. The story could have been different had Glenn Turner (30) lasted longer. Any way, it was a brilliant effort by the New Zealanders but the end was a bit tragic and for the second successive World Cup, New Zealand bowed out at the semi-final stage.

In the other semi-final against Pakistan at The Oval, the West Indies put on 293 for six, their highest total of the tournament. All their leading batsmen - Gordon Greenidge (73), Desmond Haynes (65), Vivian Richards (42) (right), Clive Lloyd (37) and Collis King (34) - showed excellent form.

The 132-run opening stand between Greenidge and Haynes remains the only century partnership for the West Indies in the semi-finals of the World Cup.

Despite a superb second-wicket partnership, producing 166 runs in 36 overs between Majid Khan (81) and Zaheer Abbas (93) - Pakistan's only century stand for the second wicket in the semi-finals of the World Cup - Pakistan failed by 43 runs to match the record West Indies World Cup total of 293. From 176 for one, Pakistan slipped to 187 for four.

Colin Croft bagged three wickets for four runs in an excellent spell of twelve balls and Pakistan collapsed from those giddy heights to 250 all out. Their last nine wickets could produce only 74 runs, thus missing an opportunity for a sensational triumph, which was within their grasp.

The final was blessed with fine weather and an all-ticket crowd of 25,000. England gambled by preferring an additional batsman, which meant, with Bob Willis injured, they had only four specialist bowlers at their disposal.

Asked to bat, West Indies lost their first four wickets for 99. The England bowlers bowled tightly and regularly beat the edge of the bats of Haynes and Greenidge and fielded magnificently, especially Randall. But they were rescued from a tottering start by Viv Richards, who played a masterly unbeaten innings of 138 off 157 balls and Collis King (86 off just 66 balls). The pair added 139 in just 77 minutes for the fifth wicket, a partnership that was to turn the match. The said stand remains the only century partnership for the fifth wicket in a World Cup final.

# CRICKET WORLD CUP
## 1979 ENGLAND

### RAJESH KUMAR

The West Indies' total of 286 for nine was just five runs short of their superb effort in the 1975 World Cup Final and it always looked a winning score.

Although captain Mike Brearley (64) and Geoff Boycott (57) put on 129 for the first wicket, they fell a long way behind the asking rate and when Brearley was dismissed, England still required 158 from the final 22 overs. Joel Garner, bowling in fading light, ripped through the order, claiming five wickets for four runs in eleven balls - his final figures being five for 38. Colin Croft (3/42) and Michael Holding (2/16) took the remaining five wickets.

England were eventually dismissed for 194, losing their last eight wickets for just eleven runs. Clive Lloyd's team retaining the World Cup by a margin of 92 runs.

Viv Richards was adjudged the Man of the Match. His blazing innings was reckoned by one commentator to be perhaps the finest of the decade.

Garner's outstanding figures remain the best ever by any bowler in the history of the World Cup finals. He (right) is one of the two bowlers to produce a five-wicket haul in the final in the history of the World Cup - the first being Australia's Gary Gilmour in the inaugural competition.

The top four wicket-takers in the tournament were - Mike Hendrick (10 at 14.90 runs apiece), Brian McKechnie (9 at 15.66), Asif Iqbal (9 at 17.44) and Chris Old (9 at 17.44).

Gordon Greenidge amassed 253 runs (ave.84.33), including a hundred and two fifties, in four innings - the most by a batsman in the 1979 competition. Just two other batsmen managed to aggregate 200-plus runs - Vivian Richards - 217 (108.50), including a hundred, in four innings and Graham Gooch - 210 (ave.52.50), including two fifties, in five innings.

Following this tournament, the ICC decided to make the competition a regular, four-yearly event, with the 1983 World Cup to be staged in England.

# CRICKET WORLD CUP
## 1983 ENGLAND

### RAJESH KUMAR

## India drops a bombshell

The West Indies, who clearly stood head and shoulders above every other side, were firm favourites to win the 1983 World Cup, the last to be sponsored by the Prudential Assurance Company. This tournament was a much more open affair than the previous two, producing a number of surprises. As in 1975 and 1979, the matches were unchanged at 60 overs per innings with a limitation of twelve overs per bowler and in each group, all sides played each other twice.

In all 27 matches were played instead of the earlier 15, to reduce the chances of a team being eliminated through a match affected by bad weather. The playing conditions empowered umpires to apply a stricter interpretation of wides and bouncers to prevent any attempts at negative bowling tactics.

Of the total matches contested over sixteen days, only three games needed the assistance of the reserve day. The top two teams in each group qualified for the semi-finals. England (20 points), who won five matches out of six, headed Group A. Their only defeat came against New Zealand (at Edgbaston), who reached the target off the penultimate ball. It was New Zealand's first limited-overs victory against England. Pakistan got the nod over New Zealand by virtue of their superior run-rate per over, both countries gaining 12 points.

As expected, the West Indies (20 points) topped the table in Group B, with just one defeat in their six encounters, that being against India (16 points), who finished runners-up, having won four matches. Since the West Indies and Australia were in Group B India were not expected to qualify for the semi-finals so it was a surprise to everyone when they reached the final.

Actually, India commenced the 1983 Prudential Cup as 66-1 outsiders. As the World Cup progressed, the Indians gained in confidence and their captain had developed into a superb all-rounder (right). The Indian supporters went through agonising moments at the picturesque ground at Tunbridge Wells. A defeat against Zimbabwe would have ruined the Indian chances to enter the semi-final for the first time. Kapil, with his magnificent knock of 175 not out, transformed a certain defeat into a surprise victory, after his side lost five wickets for 17 runs. This was the highest score ever in the World Cup at that time.

It proved a miserable tournament for Australia, who won only two matches out of six, the biggest humiliation coming in their very first encounter as they went down to Zimbabwe by 13 runs.

# CRICKET WORLD CUP
## 1983 ENGLAND

### RAJESH KUMAR

In the semi-final at Old Trafford on a warm sunny day, England made a promising start against India but were outclassed with ease and grace after the first 15 overs. The Indian bowlers, especially, Mohinder Amarnath (2 for 27), Kirti Azad (1 for 28) and Roger Binny (2 for 43) bowled well, never allowing the English batsmen to settle down and they were dismissed for 213. Kapil, who dismissed three tail-enders, finished with 3 for 35. India, like England, had an excellent start and then stumbled. However, Mohinder, with 46 in a 92-run stand with Yashpal Sharma (61) for the third wicket, set the scene for India to coast home with a significant margin of 32 balls to spare, losing only four wickets. Sandeep Patil, who had hit Bob Willis for 24 runs off one over a year before in a Test match on the same ground, batted with usual belligerence, hitting an unbeaten 51 off 32 balls with the help of eight fours. Amarnath was justifiably adjudged the Man of the Match.

In the other semi-final at The Oval, the West Indies, after five successive wins, went into the the game, quoted by bookmakers at 8-13 to retain the World Cup. They registered a comfortable eight-wicket win over Pakistan. Clive Lloyd's decision to send Pakistan in, in conditions ideal for seam and swing bowling, always looked thoroughly justified, restricting Pakistan (184-8) to just boundaries, one of them edged. Two fours in an innings remain Pakistan's fewest boundaries in a World Cup innings.

Viv Richards (80 not out) and Larry Gomes (50 not out) led the way in an unbroken stand of 132 for the third wicket, that brought victory after only 48.4 overs. West Indies at that time, had won six out of their seven games in the competition.

In the final, on a glorious summer's day, cricket enthusiasts flew in from all parts of the globe at Lord's and witnessed one of the great upsets. Lloyd, after winning the toss, invited Kapil Dev to tell his openers to bat first. Lloyd was proved correct as West Indies battery of four terrific fast bowlers (Andy Roberts, Joel Garner, Malcolm Marshall and Michael Holding) kept the Indian batsmen under pressure nearly all the time. By dismissing Sunil Gavaskar (2) in the fifth over, Roberts had claimed his first wicket in three finals - his figures being 3 for 32 off ten overs. In West Indies' World Cup final triumphs - his figures being 11-1-45-0 vs Australia in 1975 and 9-2-33-0 vs England in 1979 - both at Lord's.

A win for the West Indies looked secured when they dismissed India for 183 off 54.4 overs, which looked highly inadequate against the top-class West Indian batting on an excellent pitch. The target of 184 in the allotted 60 overs was well within their reach, even if all of them batted left-handed was the feeling when they commenced their innings.

# CRICKET WORLD CUP
## 1983 ENGLAND

### RAJESH KUMAR

The West Indians were determined to complete a hat-trick of title wins but the Indians really bowled exceptionally well. The young Indian captain, Kapil Dev must be given full credit for applying sensible pressure. The West Indies were reduced to 76 for six, and the slide continued and they were bowled out for 140. Amarnath (3 for 12), Madan lal (3 for 31) and Balwinder Sandhu (2 for 32) were the main wicket-takers for India.

The Indians registered an unexpected victory over the defending Champions, West Indies by 43 runs. An over-confident West Indian batting side, for the first time, went to pieces under pressure. India were most worthy champions, having defeated the holders, West Indies, Australia and England en route to the final. Amarnath was named the Man of the Match and became the first ever player to be adjudged Man of the Match in the semi-final and the final of the same World Cup competition.

Indian triumph on June 25, 1983 was no cricketing fluke. A fortnight earlier, they had beaten West Indies by 34 runs, successfully defending their record World Cup total of 262 for eight. So, the third World Cup that commenced in shocks ended with the greatest shock of all.

The top six run-scorers in the competition were David Gower (384 at 76.80), Viv Richards (367 at 73.40), Graeme Fowler (360 at 72.00), Zaheer Abbas (313 at 62.60), Kapil Dev (303 at 60.60) and Imran Khan (283 at 70.75).

Kapil, with 12 wickets at 20.41 in eight matches, became the first all-rounder to manage 300 runs apart from capturing ten wickets in the same World Cup competition.

Roger Binny's (right) tally, as a bowler, was the highest - 18 at 18.66, followed by Ashantha de Mel (17 at 15.58), Madan Lal (17 at 16.76), Richard Hadlee (14 at 12.85) and Vic Marks (13 at 18.92).

The Indians lifted the third Prudential World Cup. Besides the trophy and silver gilt medals for each player, India received £20,000 for their victory. The aggregate attendance in the 1983 Prudential World Cup was 232,000, compared with 158,000 in 1975 and 132,000 in 1979. It produced gate receipts of £1,950,712.

The handsome profit inspired other cricket-playing nations to bid for the next World Cup. Following the 1983 competition, the ICC had a meeting where it was decided

# CRICKET WORLD CUP
## 1983 ENGLAND

RAJESH KUMAR

to call for the tenders to be submitted by the end of the year. The fourth World Cup was awarded jointly to India and Pakistan as they guaranteed to provide sterling pounds 75,000 plus expenses to all full ICC member countries for participating in the tournament.

# CRICKET WORLD CUP
## 1987-88 INDIA & PAKISTAN

### RAJESH KUMAR

## Thrills galore as Australia lifts the Cup

The 1987-88 World Cup, sponsored by Reliance Industries, was held simultaneously in India and Pakistan in October and November 1987. It was the first World Cup to be held outside England and for the first time, no team was considered a clear-cut favourite to win the trophy.

The West Indies, the pre-tournament favourites at the three previous World Cups were clearly no longer the force they had been in the one-day game; and the defending champion, India, looked an uncertain quantity, too.

The same eight nations that had taken part in 1983, participated again in a similar format, the only change being that matches were reduced from 60 to 50 overs per side because of shorter daylight hours in the subcontinent. Accordingly, play was scheduled to commence at 9 am to help finish the games well in time. Financial penalties were imposed on countries failing to complete their 50 overs within an allotted three and a half hours' duration.

The Reliance World Cup was also the longest at that time, taking 32 days for 27 matches, which were spread around 21 venues, and the participating teams spent much of their time travelling and in airport transit lounges. The worst to suffer was Sri Lanka, who had a quite strenuous itinerary as they had to travel from one corner of Pakistan to other.

In Group A, India topped the table, followed by Australia, both teams winning five matches out of six and losing once, to each other - Australia beating India by one run at Madras on October 9, 1987. India later gained their revenge by 56 runs at Feroz Shah Kotla, Delhi on October 22. New Zealand, without their star allrounder, Richard Hadlee, finished a poor third with just two victories to their credit. Zimbabwe failed to register a single victory.

Pakistan headed the Group B table comfortably with five victories, followed by England, who registered four wins, thanks mainly to two victories over the West Indies, who were badly weakened by the absence of Malcolm Marshall. The West Indies, once the most feared opponents, went back with their reputation considerably tarnished.

Co-hosts, India and Pakistan were the favourites to contest the final but in the end, both were beaten in the semi-finals. At Gaddafi Stadium, Lahore, in the first semi-final on November 4, 1987, in front of 40,000 cricket enthusiasts, Australia (267-8) had a closer contest. Pakistan (249) seemed set to surpass Australia's total but their

# CRICKET WORLD CUP
## 1987-88 INDIA & PAKISTAN
### RAJESH KUMAR

chances were ruined by Craig McDermott, who claimed four quick wickets. His five wickets for 44 runs were the only five-wicket bowling analysis of this World Cup and he was awarded the Man of the Match for his excellent bowling. This was Pakistan's third successive World Cup semi-final defeat - the previous two being to the West Indies in 1979 & 1983.

In the second semi-final at Bombay on November 5, England (254-6), thanks mainly to Graham Gooch (115), Mike Gatting (56) and Allan Lamb (32 not out) trounced India (219) by 35 runs, despite 64 from Mohammad Azharuddidn and 30 off 22 balls from Kapil Dev. Actually, it was Eddie Hemmings' off-spin bowling (4 for 52) which finally settled the issue. Gooch was adjudged the Man of the Match for his beautiful batting.

The final was staged at Calcutta's vast Eden Gardens on November 8. Winning an important toss, Allan Border's Australians racked up an impressive 253 for five in front of 85,000 spectators, with David Boon scoring 75 and Mike Veletta (right) - 45 not out off 31 balls.

England (246-8), despite losing Tim Robinson for a first-ball duck off Craig McDermott, never gave up hope and looked on course at 135 for two but Mike Gatting (41) then fell to a reverse sweep off Australian captain, Allan Border's first ball. Bill Athey made 58 and Allan Lamb 45 and as the wickets fell, the batsmen were always behind the clock.

In the end, Australia won by just seven runs in a nail-biting finish despite a brief aggressive innings (17 off ten balls) from England's Philip DeFreitas. Their margin of victory remains the narrowest in these finals. Boon was named the Man of the Match. It was a triumph for a dedicated team effort and hard work at the nets in the heat and humidity of the sub-continent.

Graham Gooch topped the run-charts with 471 runs at an average of 58.87, including a hundred and three fifties, in eight matches, followed by David Boon - 447 (ave.55.87) in eight and Geoff Marsh - 428 (ave.61.84) in eight. McDermott, with 18 wickets at 18.94 runs apiece in eight matches, was the most successful bowler, followed by Imran Khan - 17 (ave.13.05) in seven, Patrick Patterson - 14 at 18.07 in six and Maninder Singh - 14 at 20.00 in seven.

It was a moment of pride for Australian cricket when Allan Border collected the glittering Reliance Cup from the Chief Guest in front of a mammoth crowd. Under

# CRICKET WORLD CUP
## 1987-88 INDIA & PAKISTAN

RAJESH KUMAR

his shrewd captaincy, Australia had achieved what they had not been able to do in their earlier three attempts.

The Prime Minister, Mr.Bob Hawke, summed up the feelings of the Australians when he sent the following telegram to Border: "Congratulations on a magnificent victory. Under your leadership, the Australian team has done us proud. I know how sweet this win will be for you personally."

An elated Border said after the match: "I'm ecstatic. I'm over the moon. It's a dream come true. A new era has begun in Australian cricket. We not only claimed the World Cup for the first time, but also beat two of the favourites - India and Pakistan - on our way to the final."

The 1987-88 Reliance World Cup was the most expensive tournament. ICC received Rs.3.80 crores and each participation nation, other than Zimbabwe (who got a shade less) received Rs.42.00 lakhs each. The total estimated expenditure was Rs.15 crores - India to share 2/3rd and Pakistan 1/3rd of it. India hosted 17 games and Pakistan 10.

The competition was a great success in virtually every aspect.

# CRICKET WORLD CUP
## 1991-92 AUSTRALIA & NEW ZEALAND

RAJESH KUMAR

**Imran's magical all-round wand**

The fifth World Cup, jointly hosted by Australia and New Zealand in February-March 1992, saw the return of South Africa after their apartheid exile, to international cricket. Their late inclusion, (after an appeal from Nelson Mandela) after 21 years of isolation meant a rescheduling of the programme. Their return was certainly historically significant, representing a powerful challenge to all competing teams.

The fifth World Cup, known as the Benson and Hedges World Cup, was the first to involve floodlit cricket, coloured clothing, white balls, black screens, replay screens and stump vision. Besides, the fifth World Cup was the largest ever with 39 matches - 14 of them staged in New Zealand and the remaining 25 in Australia, ten of the latter being day/night games.

This was the first World Cup to involve nine teams. The traditional teams' photograph was not taken on the field but on a ship in Sydney Harbour. As in 1987-88, the matches were again 50 overs per innings and despite there being a dozen more games than in the Reliance World Cup, the tournament was completed in 33 days and instead of being divided into groups, each side played the others once before the top four in the qualifying table played off in the semi-finals.

The highly controversial rain rule was the only major fault of the tournament, which was introduced to deal with matches affected by rain, in which the target score was proportionately reduced to the lowest-scoring overs of the team batting first.

New Zealand headed the qualifying table with 7 victories out of eight matches, collecting 14 points, followed by England (11 points), who registered five victories and lost two. South Africa, with 5 victories and 3 defeats, got 10 points. Pakistan with four wins and three losses, collected 9 points. Rain saved them at Adelaide against England when they were dismissed for 74 and the one point gained by them in the abandoned match was the one that took them above Australia in the league reckoning. They finished fourth, thanks to a vital last match win over New Zealand, which meant they qualified by a point, ahead of Australia.

The surprise packet of the tournament was New Zealand, who were not rated very highly at the commencement of the competition. The Kiwis went from strength to strength as the World Cup progressed. By the midway stage, they were being tipped to lift the World Cup. They won their first seven successive matches, including those against highly fancied opponents, before Pakistan defeated them by seven wickets at Christchurch on March 18, 1992.

# CRICKET WORLD CUP
## 1991-92 AUSTRALIA & NEW ZEALAND
RAJESH KUMAR

Pakistan again got the better of New Zealand in the first semi-final played at Eden Park, Auckland on March 21 1992 by four wickets, which was made possible by a devastating display of batting by Inzamam-ul-Haq (right) - 60 off 37 balls. Thanks to him, Pakistan made 264 for six wickets off 49 overs. It was heartbreaking for New Zealand captain Martin Crowe, the most consistent batsman of the tournament, who made 91 off 83 balls in New Zealand's 262 for seven, taking his tournament aggregate to 456 (ave.114.00), including a hundred and four fifties - the highest by a batsman in the competition.

In the second semi-final at the Sydney Cricket Ground on March 22, the 'highest scoring overs' rain regulation spoiled the prospect of an exciting finish. Put into bat, England, with the help of Graeme Hick (83) posted 252 for six wickets off 45 overs. In response, South Africa (232 for six off 43 overs) were progressing nicely towards the target before the rain came in the losing stages and snatched a possible victory from them.

In the final at Melbourne Cricket ground on March 25, after three semi-final defeats and a disastrous start in this tournament, Pakistan won the Benson and Hedges World Cup, defeating England by 22 runs before a record Australian limited-overs crowd of 87,182.

Pakistan, electing to bat after winning the toss, made 249 for six, with 153 of those coming in their final 20 overs. The leading scorers for Pakistan being the two veterans - Captain Imran Khan (72) and Javed Miandad (58), who had put on 139 runs in 31 overs after both the openers, Aamir Sohail (4) and Rameez Raja (8) were dismissed by Derek Pringle. At 197 for four, Pakistan hadn't yet got out of trouble but the 52-run stand between Inzamam-ul-Haq (42 off 35 balls) and Wasim Akram (33 off 19 balls) got them to a reasonably good total. Pringle bowled well, capturing 3 for 22 off ten overs.

In response, England (227) never really mounted a serious challenge after being reduced to 69 for four, despite a brave 62 off 70 balls from Neil Fairbrother and they never really looked like overhauling their opponent's total. Akram, who claimed three wickets conceding 49 runs, apart from a quick-fire 33 was adjudged the Man of the Match. Mushtaq Ahmed (3 for 41) and Aaqib Javed (2 for 27) bowled splendidly and got away with economical stints.

Javed Miandad finished with 437 runs (ave.62.42), including five fifties, in nine matches - the second highest tally behind Martin Crowe's 456.

# CRICKET WORLD CUP

**1991-92** AUSTRALIA &
NEW ZEALAND

RAJESH KUMAR

Four top wicket-takers in the competition were Wasim Akram (18 at 18.77), Ian Botham (16 at 19.12), Mushtaq Ahmed (16 at 19.43) and Chris Harris (16 at 21.37).

Sir Colin Cowdrey, President of the ICC, presented Imran Khan with the Benson and Hedges World Cup, a waterford crystal globe.  The receipts for this World Cup were Australian dollars $2 million.

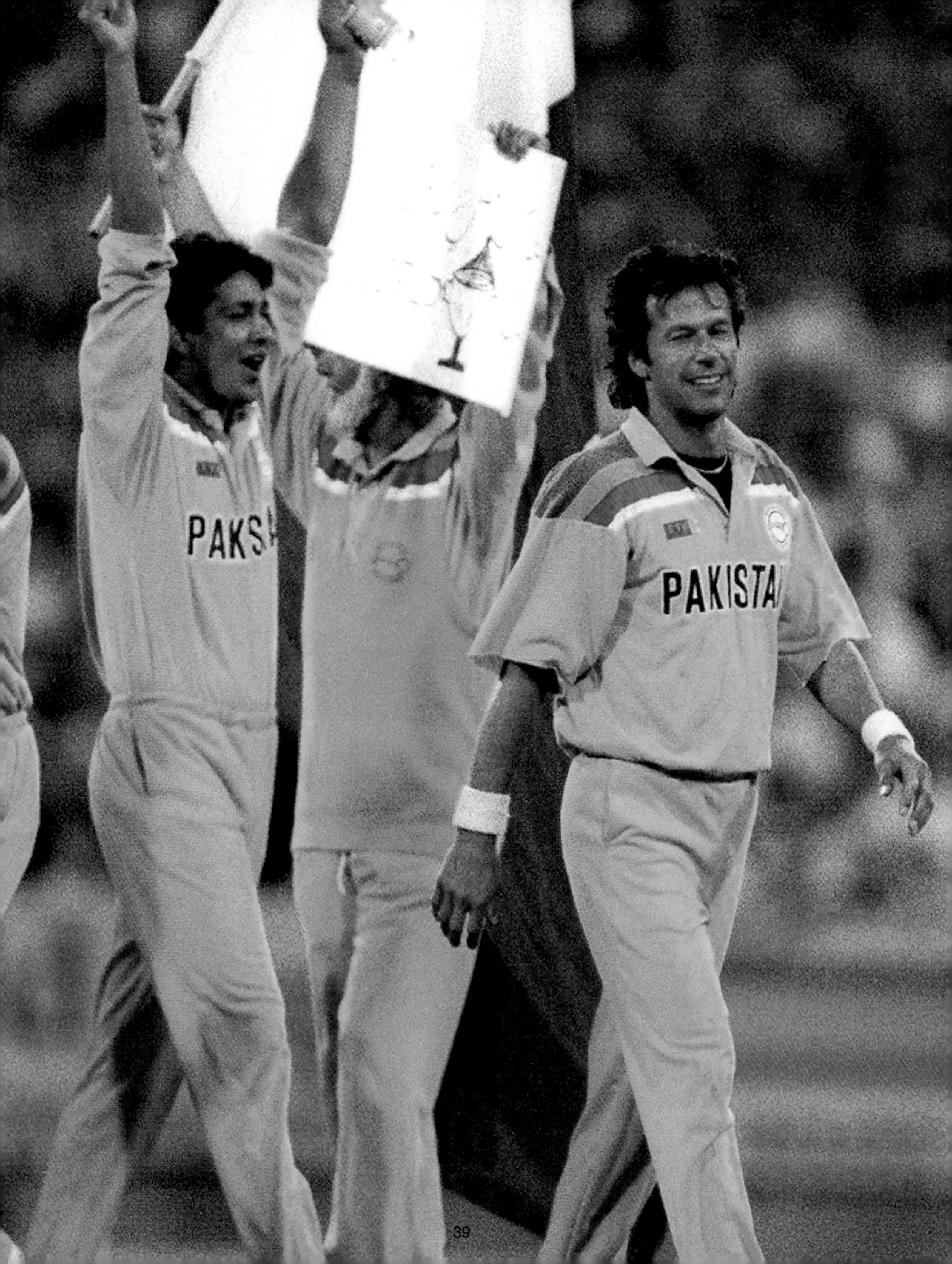
PAKS
PAKISTA

# CRICKET WORLD CUP
## 1995-96 INDIA
## PAKISTAN &
## SRI LANKA

RAJESH KUMAR

## Arvinda behind Sri Lanka's joy and glory

Sponsored by Wills, the sixth World Cup involved more host countries (three) - India, Pakistan and Sri Lanka, more teams (12) with Holland, Kenya and United Arab Emirates joining the fray and more grounds (26) than any of its predecessors.

Despite the cancellation of two matches, Group A comprising of Australia, West Indies, Zimbabwe, Sri Lanka, India and Kenya outstripped Group B consisting of New Zealand, South Africa, England, United Arab Emirates, Pakistan and Holland in terms of competitive games, besides providing all the four semi-finalists.

Apart from the lacklustre opening ceremony, the tournament was beset by problems as two matches could not take place (a fortnight before the start of the tournament, the Tamil Tigers exploded a bomb in the center of Colombo, persuading Australia and West Indies to forfeit their games against Sri Lanka), another was brought to a premature end by crowd trouble, and too many of the qualifying games were far from satisfactory, producing one-sided results, as commercial considerations seemed to outweigh all else.

Kenya's victory over West Indies at Poona by 73 runs, was one of international cricket's greatest reversals. Put into bat by Richie Richardson, Kenya made 166, Steve Tikolo scoring 29 and Hitesh Modi 26. Defending a modest total, they dismissed West Indies (93) for their lowest World Cup total. For Kenya, all their bowlers bowled magnificently. Maurice Odumbe (3 for 15) and Rajab Ali (3 for 17) were their leading bowlers.

The first semi-final between India and Sri Lanka at Eden Gardens, Kolkata on March 13, 1996 was the first major cricket match to be awarded by default. The match started sensationally when both Sri Lankan openers - Jayasuriya (1) and Kaluwitharana (0) fell in Srinath's opening over but Aravinda de Silva (66 off 47 balls) counter-attacked with a 32-ball fifty. He was assisted by Mahanama (58 retired hurt), Ranatunga (35), Tillekeratne (32) and Vaas (23), enabling Sri Lanka to reach 251 for eight. In reply, India after making 98 for one at one stage collapsed dramatically and lost their next seven wickets for just 22 runs. After the dismissal of Tendulkar (65) and Manjrekar (25), the wickets fell at regular intervals when sections of crowd, estimated at 100,000, lit fires and hurled missiles at the fielders.

# CRICKET WORLD CUP
## 1995-96 INDIA
## PAKISTAN &
## SRI LANKA

RAJESH KUMAR

Clive Lloyd, the match referee called off play for 20 minutes to allow tempers to cool but when more bottles landed on the ground after the players returned, he decided to abandon play and awarded the game to Sri Lanka.

Mohali staged its first illuminated international between Australia and West Indies on March 14. This semi-final encounter produced the best contest of the tournament. Batting first, Australia, after losing four early wickets at 15, recovered from a desperate position, thanks to the sensible batting of 'young guns' - Stuart Law (72) and Michael Bevan (69), who put on 138 runs in 32 overs. The pair, with assistance from Ian Healy (31 off 28 balls) took Australia (207 for eight) towards a respectable total. Ambrose (2 for 26) and Bishop (2 for 35) bowled splendidly and did not allow any liberty to the Australian batsmen.

In reply, the West Indies, with 165 for two at one stage, wilted under the pressure and lost their last eight wickets for 37 runs in 50 balls with Shane Warne, claiming three wickets for six runs off three overs. He was justifiably adjudged the Man of the Match. Thanks to his match-winning figures of four for 36, Australia won by 5 runs. Chanderpaul (80), Lara (45) and captain Richardson (49 not out) played reasonably well but after their dismissal, the Australian bowlers had the upper hand in the proceedings.

The final was played at Gaddafi Stadium, Lahore between Australia and Sri Lanka on March 17. It was the first occasion in the history of Pakistan cricket that a Limited-overs International was played under lights. Put into bat, Australian captain, Mark Taylor showed his class and runs flowed from his bat freely, especially on the leg side and once lifted Vaas over square leg for six. The second-wicket stand of 101 runs between Taylor (74) and Ponting (45), and an unfinished partnership of 36 between Bevan (36 not out) and Paul Reiffel (13 not out) for the eight wicket, enabled Australia to register 241 for seven. Aravinda de Silva, with three for 42, was the most successful bowler.

As in the semi-final match against India, the Sri Lankan openers - Sanath Jayasuriya - Right - (9) and Romesh Kaluwitharana (6) once again failed to put a decent score on the board. But Gurusinha (65), Aravinda de Silva (107 not out) and Arjuna Ranatunga (47 not out) ensured a convincing victory for their side by seven wickets. Apart from becoming the first host team to win the World Cup trophy, Sri Lanka became the first team to win a World Cup final batting second.

# CRICKET WORLD CUP

## 1995-96 INDIA
## PAKISTAN &
## SRI LANKA

RAJESH KUMAR

They were the fifth country to win the World Cup in successive tournaments - the first four being West Indies (1975 & 1979), India (1983), Australia (1987) and Pakistan (1992).

Aravinda de Silva (right), with a superb all-round performance - 107 not out, three wickets and two catches, was adjudged the Man of the Match. He remains the only all-rounder to post a fifty-plus and bag three wickets in a World Cup final.

Jayasuriya (221 runs at 36.83, 7 wickets at 33.00 and five catches in six matches) was deservingly named the Player of the tournament. He received an Audi A4 motor car. The top three run-scorers were Sachin Tendulkar (523 at 87.16 in seven matches), Mark Waugh (484 at 80.66 in seven) and Aravinda de Silva (448 at 89.60 in six). Just two bowlers could take 13 wickets or more in the tournament - Anil Kumble - 15 at 18.73 in seven matches and Waqar Younis - 13 at 19.46 in six.

Winners, Sri Lanka received £30,000 and runners-up Australia got £20,000 while each losing semi-finalists (India and West Indies) received £10,000. A fee of £250,000 to each of the competing Test countries was paid and the hosts pocketed a profit of almost US $50 million.

The Wills World Cup was presented to Ranatunga by Pakistan's Prime Minister Benazir Bhutto.

Sri Lanka came of age in spectacular fashion in the sixth World Cup which they helped to stage with India and Pakistan. They proved worthy winners, defeating Australia by seven wickets in the final, to provide a memorable finale to a tournament beset by problems.

# CRICKET WORLD CUP
## 1999 ENGLAND

### RAJESH KUMAR

## The Waughs win the battle

Since its inception in 1975 in England, the World Cup grew in stature and went from strength to strength and after successfully hosting the three successive tournaments in 1975, 1979 and 1983 by England, the International Cricket Council brought the World Cup back to England after a gap of 16 years.

The ICC Cricket World Cup featured twelve teams and 42 matches, (including two in Edinburgh and one each in Dublin, Cardiff and Amsterdam) apart from using 21 different host venues in five countries and US $ one million in prize money, which was more than three times that ever offered before. The seventh World Cup was the first without a company tag. NatWest, Vodafone, Pepsi and Emirates Airlines were the 'Global Partners' besides a number of official supporters.

Apart from the nine full ICC members, the top three sides - Scotland, Bangladesh and Kenya - from last year's ICC Trophy, participated in the competition and played for a permanent World Cup trophy, crafted in silver and gilt, designed and manufactured in London by Garrard, the Crown Jewellers, valued at more than £27,000.

The tournament was split into two groups of six. Because of their outstanding one-day international record in recent years prior to the World Cup, apart from having an enviable line-up of world-class all-rounders, the South Africans were the pre-tournament favourites. They were placed with holders Sri Lanka in the tougher looking Group A, the other four teams being India, England, Zimbabwe and Kenya and Group B comprised of Australia, New Zealand, West Indies, Pakistan, Bangladesh and Scotland.

They each played the other five nations in their group with the top three teams in each group progressing to the super six round taking with them the points scored against the other successful teams in their group. The top four at the end of the Super six phase competed in the semi-finals.

The Duckworth/Lewis method of setting revised targets were applied in the games caused by interruptions. According to John Stern of The Times, London, it was Steve Waugh's innings of 120 from 110 balls against South Africa at Headingley, Leeds, which dragged his team into the semi-finals by the skin of their teeth. "Waugh's innings was one of the finest the World Cup has seen for its relevance as much as its willpower and skill."

47

# CRICKET WORLD CUP
## 1999 ENGLAND

### RAJESH KUMAR

Pakistan and New Zealand contested the first semi-final at Old Trafford, Manchester on June 16, 1999. Winning the toss and batting first, New Zealand totalled 241 for seven, with useful contributions from Matt Horne (35), Captain Stephen Fleming (41), Roger Twose (46), Chris Cairns (44 not out) with extras being the top scorer (47). But New Zealand's hopes of playing their first World Cup final were dashed by Saeed Anwar (113 not out) and Wajahatullah Wasti (84), who batted with complete assurance, putting on 194 for the first wicket, which was a record for the first wicket at that time in World Cup matches.

Geoff Allott, who could not take a single wicket in this match, failed to extend his record for the number of wickets (20) in a World Cup. Pakistan (242/1) won by a convincing margin of nine wickets and reached the Final. Shoaib Akhtar (3/55) was named the Man of the Match - his only award in the World Cup.

The second semi-final between Australia and South Africa played at Edgbaston, Birmingham on June 17 resulted in the World Cup's first ever tie. Since Australia had finished higher than South Africa after the conclusion of the Super Six, with an equal number of points and a net run rate only fractionally better than the third-placed South Africa, the result (tie) was as good as a win for Australia. Both sides were dismissed identically for 213.

Captain Steve Waugh (56) and Michael Bevan (65) posted 50-plus runs for Australia. Pollock bowled quite well to claim five wickets for 36 runs (his only five-wicket haul in the World Cup) while Allan Donald finished with four wickets for 32 runs but it was Shane Warne, who found his rhythm immediately with figures of four for 29. Warne was named the Man of the Match.

Tim De Lisle, covering the match for Wisden Cricketers' Almanack, described it as: "This was not merely the match of the tounament: it must have been the best one-day international of the 1483 so far played. The essence of the one-day game is a close finish, and this was by far the most significant to finish in the closest way of all - with both teams all out for the same score."

Australia outplayed Pakistan and won the seventh World Cup (the 200th World Cup match), with a convincing margin of eight wickets at Lord's on June 20, 1999, which was the most one-sided result of all World Cup finals and there were barely four and half hours of cricket. After the two thrilling encounters between Australia and South Africa, the final was a big let-down.

# CRICKET WORLD CUP
## 1999 ENGLAND

### RAJESH KUMAR

Wasim Akram won the toss and opted to bat and after a delayed start by 30 minutes, the Pakistani batsmen struggled against the accurate Australian bowling of Glenn McGrath (2 for 13 off nine overs), Paul Reiffel (1 for 29 off ten overs), Tom Moody (2 for 17) and Shane Warne (4 for 33) and were dismissed for a paltry 132, which remains a lowest total in a World Cup final. Australia, in response, needed only 121 balls to reach the target, with Adam Gilchrist scoring a beautiful innings of 54 off 36 balls. As in the semi-final, Warne was adjudged Man of the Match. With a tally of 20 wickets at 18.05 in ten matches in the tournament, he had emulated Allott. Both tied each other for most wickets captured in the competition.

Australia became the second team after West Indies to lift the World Cup on two occasions and the best Test side in the World added the title as the best one-day international team.

The top run-getters in the 1999 World Cup were Rahul Dravid (461 at 65.85), Steve Waugh (398 at 79.60), Sourav Ganguly (379 at 54.14) and Mark Waugh (375 at 41.66).

Lance Klusener (right), with 281 runs (ave.140.50) and 17 wickets (ave.20.59) in nine matches, got the car as the player of the tournament. Champions Australia received US $300,000, the runners-up, Pakistan US $150,000 and each of the losing semi-finalists, South Africa and New Zealand US $100,000.

# CRICKET WORLD CUP
## 2002-03 ZIMBABWE SOUTH AFRICA & KENYA

RAJESH KUMAR

## The invincible Aussies

The 2003 Cricket World Cup, featuring 14 teams (the largest number in the history at that time) was played in South Africa, Zimbabwe and Kenya from February 9 to March 23. For the first time, the World Cup was held in Africa.

The tournament was the eighth Cricket World Cup, won by Australia, beating India in the final. They had won all their eleven fixtures in this World Cup. Having won in 1987 and 1999, this was Australia's third World Cup triumph, the only nation to accomplish the feat thrice.

There had been a number of pre-tournament controversies, including the security and political situation in Zimbabwe. Two Zimbabwean players, captain Andy Flower and Henry Olonga (the former white, the latter black) wore black armbands for their opening game to protest Robert Mugabe's presidency. They later expanded on their stand by calling their act as "mourning the death of democracy in Zimbabwe".

Australian star player Shane Warne was sent home in disgrace, only the day before their opening game, after testing positive for a banned substance. Warne, in his plea, said he had taken a pill, advised by his mother, to help him lose weight.

England faced a great deal of domestic pressure to boycott their match in Zimbabwe due to the political climate and security fears, and after some prevarication - initially announcing that they would play - did not play, citing fears for the players' safety. Similarly, New Zealand decided against playing in Kenya because of security fears and hosts were awarded the match and after defeating a food-poisoning stricken Sri Lankan team, they qualified for the semi-finals.

Fourteen teams played in the 2003 Cricket World Cup, retaining the format implemented in the 1999 World Cup. In the first round, they were divided into two groups of seven teams. The best three of each group qualified for the "Super Six", carrying the results against other qualifiers from their group to that round. The top four teams qualified for the semi-finals, and the winners of those matches played the final.

First Semi-final: March 18, 2003 Australia vs Sri Lanka. Winning an important toss and batting first, Australia racked up 212 for seven against accurate Sri Lankan

53

# CRICKET WORLD CUP
## 2002-03 ZIMBABWE
RAJESH KUMAR
## SOUTH AFRICA
## & KENYA

bowling, thanks mainly to a superb unbeaten knock of 91 off 118 balls from Andrew Symonds. Chaminda Vaas bagged three wickets, conceding 34 runs off his ten overs. Adam Gilchrist (22), despite being given not out by the on-field umpire while attempting to sweep off Aravinda de Silva, got a thin edge on to his pad, was caught behind. He had paused for a while but walked back to the pavilion, setting an example for all cricketers.

Australia's fast-bowling attack then kept the Sri Lankan batsmen under pressure nearly all the time, with Brett Lee taking three early wickets and Glenn McGrath taking one. Sri Lanka were reduced to 123 for seven after 38.1 overs when rain interrupted. Australia won the match convincingly by 48 runs under Duckworth-Lewis method.

Second Semi-final at Kingsmead, Durban: March 20, 2003 India vs Kenya. Batting first on winning the toss, India, after the dismissal of Virender Sehwag (33), consolidated their innings with a 103-run stand for the second wicket between Sachin Tendulkar (83) and Sourav Ganguly (111 off 114 balls), ensuring a respectable total of 270 for four off 50 overs. His match-winning hundred was his third in this World Cup and the 22nd and the last of his ODI career.

Chasing India's score, the Kenyan batsmen, except captain Steve Tikolo (56), could not get going while facing the Indian speedsters - Zaheer Khan (right) (3/14), Javagal Srinath (1/11) and Ashish Nehra (2/11). Kenya, the only non-Test-playing team to appear in a World Cup semi-final, got dismissed for 179, losing by 91 runs.

Final - March 24, 2003 - Australia vs India - the first instance of both the teams contesting against each other in a World Cup final. India won the toss, and Sourav Ganguly, strangely, asked Australia to bat. Bringing up Australia's first century opening stand in a World Cup final in the fourteenth over, Adam Gilchrist, who had been aggressive, scoring 57 off 48 balls, left with Australia at 105 for one. Matthew Hayden, looking somewhat impressive than he had throughout the competition, soon followed for 37, leaving Australia at 125 for two. Harbhajan Singh had dismissed both the openers. Javagal Srinath (10-0-87-0) produced his worst bowling figures in terms of runs conceded. The final turned out to be his last ODI.

Captain Ricky Ponting (140 off 121 balls - the highest individual score in a World Cup final at that time) and Damien Martyn (playing with a broken thumb) then shared an unbroken partnership of 234 at a run-rate of 7.75 for the third wicket, the only double century stand in a World Cup final. Ponting and Martyn (88 not out off 84 balls) commenced batting in a style, dominating the proceedings, rotated the strike

# CRICKET WORLD CUP
## 2002-03 ZIMBABWE
## SOUTH AFRICA
## & KENYA

RAJESH KUMAR

efficiently. The pair had managed 109 runs in the last ten overs. The final Australian total of 359 for two was their second highest ever at that time in ODI history and remains the only 300-plus total in a final of the World Cup.

Ponting's marvellous innings, providing his team an upper hand even before India had batted, was embellished with eight sixes, all in the arc between long-on and square-leg - a record in a World Cup final, which was emulated by Adam Gilchrist, during his outstanding knock of 149 off 104 balls in the final vs Sri Lanka at Bridgetown on April 28, 2007.

The Australian score looked impregnable, especially after Sachin Tendulkar (4) was out in the first over off Glenn McGrath, who had completed the caught and bowled dismissal. Virender Sehwag's run-a-ball superb fifty provided India respectability as they maintained an excellent scoring rate.

However, the rain proved fleeting, and India's hopes were dashed when Sehwag was run out by Darren Lehmann for 82 off 81 balls. India's batsmen continued to throw wickets away in the chase and were finally bowled out for 234 giving Australia an emphatic victory by a record margin (in World Cup finals thus so far) of 125 runs, underlining their dominance of the tournament. The 88-run fourth-wicket partnership between Sehwag and Dravid (47) was India's highest for any wicket in a World Cup final at that time.

Glenn McGrath (3/52), Brett Lee (2/31) and Andrew Symonds (2/7) were the main wicket-takers for Australia. The Indian skipper's decision to bowl first was criticised by former players and journalists.

Ponting, who set a record individual score by a captain at the World Cup, was named the Man of the Match and Sachin Tendulkar, for his demolition of bowling attacks, was named Player of the Tournament. Tendulkar's tally of 673 (ave.61.18) in eleven matches, including a hundred and six fifties, is an all-time record for most runs in a World Cup competition.

# CRICKET WORLD CUP
## 2006-07 WEST INDIES
### KERSI MEHER-HOMJI

## Caribbean misadventures

What a sharp contrast between the West Indies team making their debut in World Cup 1975 and the West Indies organizers hosting the World Cup in the Caribbean 32 years later! Their debut as players was brilliant – winning the inaugural World Cup. However, their hosting the World Cup 2006-07 was little short of disastrous ending with a big anti-climax in the rain-spoilt Final between Australia and Sri Lanka in Barbados on April 28, 2007.

The quality of cricket in World Cup 2006-07 was outstanding – especially by champions Australia – but the organizing of the international event left something to be desired. In all, the tournament dragged on for 47 days, as long as the last Olympic games and football World Cup put together. It was a duration dictated by the increase from 14 teams in 2003 to 16 and the introduction of reserve days in case of bad weather. As it was, only one of the 51 matches carried over the second day.

The countries were divided in four Groups:
**Group A:** Australia, South Africa, Netherlands, Scotland.
**Group B:** India, Sri Lanka, Bangladesh, Bermuda.
**Group C:** England, New Zealand, Kenya, Canada.
**Group D:** West Indies, Pakistan, Zimbabwe, Ireland.

The early exit of glamour teams India and Pakistan made the locals lose interest in attending matches. Most of the time the stands were less than half full and so were the hotels. The nine governments which make up the Caribbean lost millions of dollars. The high cost of ticket purchase also led to poor attendances.

The tragedy of this World Cup came within a week of its launch. The sudden death of Bob Woolmer, the respected Pakistan coach and former England batsman in his Kingston hotel room hours after Pakistan was eliminated, shocked the cricket world. Four days later, the Jamaican police declared that Woolmer was murdered. Later it was stated that Woolmer, a diabetic with heart problems, had died of natural causes.

Despite these mishaps, the quality of cricket was high. Here are some of the World Cup records set during this World Cup in 2007:

Australia's Matthew Hayden (right) reached his century against South Africa at Basseterre in 66 balls on March 24. This was later surpassed by Kevin O'Brien (113 off 63 balls) with his 50-ball century for Ireland against England at Bengaluru on March 2, 2011).

# CRICKET WORLD CUP
## 2006-07 WEST INDIES

KERSI MEHER-HOMJI

Australia's Shane Watson scored 145 runs in the tournament at a strike rate of 170.58 (minimum100 runs).

South Africa's Herschelle Gibbs (right) hit 6 sixes in an over off Holland's Daan van Bunge at Basseterre on March 16. This was the first such instance in any international match.

Sri Lanka's fast bowler Lasith Malinga, the one with gold-tinted locks, took four wickets in four balls against South Africa at Providence, Guyana on March 28. Just like Gibbs' six sixes in an over 12 days earlier, this was the first instance in any international.

India totalled 5 for 413 against Bermuda at Port-of-Spain on March 19. This was then the highest team total in a World Cup match. [This record was later broken by Australia scoring 6 for 417 against Afghanistan at Perth on March 4, 2015].

India won the match (mismatch?) at Port-of-Spain by 257 runs, a record margin of victory in a One-Day International. [This record was later broken by Australia defeating Afghanistan by 275 runs at Perth on March 4, 2015].

Overall, Australia was the strongest team in this World Cup. They won all their 11 matches, scoring over 300 runs whenever they batted first before the rain interrupted Final in which they totalled 4 for 281 in 38 overs.

Dynamic captain Ricky Ponting led Australia to her third successive World Cup triumph thus bettering Clive Lloyd's win record in the 1975 and 1979 World Cups.

Four of Australia's batsmen figured in the top ten run-scorers list and four of their bowlers in top seven wicket-takers list. Hayden (659 runs at 73.22) was on top of the batting list, having scored 111 runs more than the next best – Sri Lanka's Mahela Jayawardene.

Australia's Glenn McGrath was on top of the bowling list (26 wickets, a World Cup record, at 13.73) and was the Player of the Series in this World Cup. The next best were Sri Lanka's Muttiah Muralitharan, 23 wickets at 15.26 and Australia's Shaun Tate, 23 wickets at 20.30.

Four thrillers were played in this World Cup.

**Ireland against Zimbabwe at Kingston:** The match resulted in the third tie in World Cup history. Sent in to bat Ireland, making its World Cup debut, scored 9 for

# CRICKET WORLD CUP
## 2006-07 WEST INDIES

### KERSI MEHER-HOMJI

221. Zimbabwe started well but lost their last five wickets for 18 runs and the match was tied.

**South Africa against Sri Lanka at Guyana:** South Africa won by one wicket with four balls in hand.

**England against Sri Lanka at Antigua:** Sri Lanka won by two runs off the last ball of the match.

**England against West Indies at Bridgetown:** Off the fifth ball of the final over from Dwayne Bravo, Stuart Broad hit two runs and England won by one wicket.

Teams to enter the Super Eight stage were Australia, South Africa, Sri Lanka, Bangladesh, New Zealand, England, West Indies and Ireland. In the semi-finals Sri Lanka beat New Zealand by 81 runs at Kingston and Australia defeated South Africa by seven wickets at St Lucia. Thus the two strongest teams in the tournament, Australia and Sri Lanka, clashed in the Final at Bridgetown, Barbados.

This match could be described as the Dr Jekyll and Mr Hyde of World Cup cricket. Adam Gilchrist (right) batted magnificently to score 149 off 104 deliveries, the highest of the six centuries scored in a Final and the first and the only one by an opening batsman. He smashed eight sixes to equal the record for any World Cup and led Australia to their third consecutive World Cup triumph, a record.

However, this Final had its downside. The poor organisation turned this Final into a farce. Rain delayed the commencement of the match from 9.30 am to 12.15. The recalculation made it a 38 overs match. Although nearly three hours were lost, only 24 overs were reduced.

Inspired by Gilchrist's magnificent 149 including eight sixes, Australia scored 4 for 281 in the allocated 38 overs. When on 31 he was dropped by Dilhara Fernando. Relieved, he smacked Fernando for 4, 4 and 6 in that over. That six very nearly smashed the fire engine next to the 3Ws Stand at long-on. To help him hit straight, he held a squash ball in his left batting glove. Although not illegal, it aroused controversy.

With Sanath Jayasuriya and Kumar Sangakkara batting brilliantly, Sri Lanka was one down for 123 at one stage and in the hunt to chase Australia's total. But there was one more rain interruption when Sri Lanka was on 3 for 149 off 24.5 overs. Two more overs were deducted, reducing Sri Lanka's win target to 269 runs off 36 overs.

# CRICKET WORLD CUP
## 2006-07 WEST INDIES
### KERSI MEHER-HOMJI

To me this appeared a fair calculation as Sri Lanka had to score 13 less runs in two less overs. But they had to bat in increasing darkness and on a wet pitch. Their reliable batsman Tillekeratne Dilshan was run out after he slipped going for a run.

The umpires and match referee Jeff Crowe believed that 36 overs of Sri Lanka's innings had to be completed for a result. So intent were they [umpires and referee] on their Duckworth/Lewis calculations that they were oblivious to the fact that the result was going to be achieved on the day the moment 20 overs had been bowled.

Crowe admitted later: "It was a mistake on our behalf. I should have known the rules. It was a human error."

After 33 overs Sri Lanka was offered light a second time and accepted it at 6.08 pm. Eight minutes later the players returned to the field on a damp and dark evening to complete three overs of spin. Sri Lanka managed 8 for 215 in 36 overs and lost by 53 runs by D/L method.

The closing ceremony was almost lost in darkness and the administrators were booed by the crowd. According to Tony Cozier, the Final "turned into a protracted nightmare." Simon Barnes summed up the match in *The Times* as "the worst sporting event in history."

The ebullient Gilchrist was made Man of the Match and the evergreen 37 year-old Glenn McGrath (26 wickets at an average of 13.73) voted Player of the Series. It was McGrath's swansong in international cricket. He left the scene with three World Cup records; 26 wickets in this tournament, his overall tally of 71 scalps and the best bowling spell of 7 for 15 against Namibia at Potchefstroom on February 27, 2003.

# CRICKET WORLD CUP

## 2010-11 INDIA
## SRI LANKA
## BANGLADESH

### KERSI MEHER-HOMJI

## Dhoni lifts sixes and the World Cup

Euphoria sums up the feelings of a billion Indians when MS Dhoni's men won the World Cup in Mumbai, India on April 2, 2011.

It was quite the opposite of the previous World Cup in the Caribbean when stands were less than half full. In most of the matches in this tournament, the Stadia were overfull, especially when India played. Sachin Tendulkar, Virender Sehwag, skipper MS Dhoni and Yuvraj Singh were the superstars who attracted spectators from far and near.

Previously India's only World Cup win was in 1983 at Lord's. The Final for this World Cup was at Mumbai's Wankhede Stadium where over 42,000 cheered every Indian run and every Indian appeal for a wicket with gusto. Not to forget the billion of them glued to their or their neighbours' TV set.

In 1983, India's World Cup win was miraculous, like winning a lottery. "What, beating the mighty Windies all set for their hat-trick of wins? You must be joking!" was the general reaction when India entered the 1983 Final.

For the 2011 Final, winning was a dream but not a pipe dream. The home supporters were quietly confident but still anything can happen in cricket with Sri Lanka's all-round excellence. And when it happened … but I am going ahead of the story.

Learning from their mistake in having 16 countries compete in four Groups in the previous World Cup the current one staged in the Indian subcontinent had only 14 countries in two groups.

**Group A:** Australia, New Zealand, Pakistan, Sri Lanka, Zimbabwe, Canada. Kenya.

**Group B:** England, South Africa, West Indies, India, Bangladesh, Ireland, Netherlands.

Players from the Indian subcontinent dominated in batting, bowling, fielding and wicket-keeping in this World Cup:

# CRICKET WORLD CUP
## 2010-11 INDIA
## SRI LANKA
## BANGLADESH

**KERSI MEHER-HOMJI**

Sri Lanka's Tillakaratne Dilshan (500 runs at an average of 62.50), India's Sachin Tendulkar (482 at 53.55) and Kumar Sangakkara (465 at 93.00) were the leading run-scorers. All three appeared in nine matches each.

The top individual score was by India's Virender Sehwag, 175 runs off 140 balls against Bangladesh at Mirpur.

Leading wicket-takers were Pakistan's Shahid Afridi (21 wickets at an average of 12.85) and India's Zaheer Khan (21 wickets at 18.76).

Sri Lanka's Lasith Malinga was one of the two bowlers to take a hat-trick, against Kenya at Colombo (RPS). Kemar Roach from West Indies also took a hat-trick, against Netherlands at Delhi.

Sri Lanka's Ajantha Mendis was the most economical bowler in the tournament, conceding 3.14 runs per over (minimum qualification: 5 wickets).

Sri Lanka's Mahela Jayawardene took most catches, eight in nine matches and Sri Lanka's wicket keeper Kumar Sangakkara made most dismissals, 14 (10 catches and four stumpings) in nine matches.

Apart from statistics this World Cup will be remembered for five nail-biters, four of them involving England.

Highest scoring World Cup tie was played between England and India at Bengaluru. This was the fourth and last tie in the World Cup. With two runs needed for an English win off the last ball they could take only one and the match was tied.

In another thriller at Bengaluru against Ireland, England totalled 8 for 327. Ireland's Kevin O'Brien (right) hit 100 off 50 balls with six sixes leading Ireland to win by three wickets in the final over.

England's luck changed at Chennai when they defeated South Africa by six runs with 14 balls remaining.

In reply to England's 225, Bangladesh was 8 for 169 in Chittagong. But tail-enders Mohammad Mahmudullah and Shafiul Islam took Bangladesh to a surprise two wicket win with an over to spare.

# CRICKET WORLD CUP

## 2010-11 INDIA
## SRI LANKA
## BANGLADESH

### KERSI MEHER-HOMJI

Against South Africa at Nagpur India was floating at 1 for 267. It was Tendulkar's sixth World Cup century and 99th in all internationals. But his dismissal started a collapse and India was all out for 296. South Africa won by three wickets with two balls remaining.

India started her campaign with flourish beating Bangladesh by 87 runs at Mirpur on February 19. This was the first World Cup match hosted in Bangladesh and 26,728 spectators enjoyed the run feast, watching breath-taking centuries from Sehwag (175 runs with 14 fours and five sixes off 140 balls) and Virat Kohli (100 not out off 83 balls) as India totalled 4 for 370. This was a spectacular World Cup debut for Kohli. For Bangladesh, opening batsman Tamim Iqbal and skipper Shakib Al Hasan scored fifties but with fast-medium Munaf Patel taking 4 for 48 they ended up at 9 for 283.

Teams to enter the quarter-finals were Pakistan, Sri Lanka, Australia and New Zealand from Group A; and South Africa, India, England and West Indies from Group B. Of these Pakistan, India, New Zealand and Sri Lanka made it to the semi-final.

In the first semi-final Sri Lanka defeated New Zealand by five wickets at Colombo (RPS) to advance to their second consecutive World Cup Final. It was New Zealand's sixth semi-final loss out of six. With Scott Styris scoring a patient 57 off 77 balls, the Kiwis were going well at 5 for 204 but their last five wickets tumbled for 13 runs and were dismissed for 217 in 48.5 overs.

Dilshan (73 runs) and skipper Sangakkara (54) added 120 runs for the second wicket and Sri Lanka reached the target with 13 balls to spare. For his sparkling fifty which included seven fours and a six and taking three catches, Sangakkara (right) was made Man of the Match.

The second semi-final at Mohali was between arch rivals India and Pakistan. It was Tendulkar's lucky day as he was dropped four times when on 27, 45, 70 and 81; three of them off Shahid Afridi. Saeed Ajmal finally had Tendulkar caught by Afridi, 15 runs short of his 100th international century. His 85 had come off 115 balls and included 11 fours. Suresh Raina attacked with gusto to score a breezy and unbeaten 36 with three fours. Wahab Riaz (5 for 46) bowled effectively as India finished with 9 for 260.

Pakistan started briskly but India fielded with alacrity to slow down the run rate. Although Misbah-ul-Haq top scored with 56 he started slowly, leaving big hitting till

71

# CRICKET WORLD CUP

## 2010-11 INDIA

### KERSI MEHER-HOMJI

## SRI LANKA
## BANGLADESH

the end. It was too little, too late and Pakistan lost by 29 runs. Tendulkar was adjudged Man of the Match.

The two strongest teams in the tournament, India and Sri Lanka, entered the Final. The match started on a controversial note as the toss was disputed. Skipper Kumar Sangakkara's initial call was drowned out by the crowd noise.

Then it was the highs and lows of India's fast-medium bowler Zaheer Khan which highlighted the first hour of this fluctuating Final. Zaheer opened with three consecutive maidens and had Upul Tharanga caught by Sehwag in a magnificent spell of 5-3-6-1. In sharp contrast Zaheer was smacked for 17 and 18 runs in his ninth and tenth overs.

After losing both their openers for 60, Sangakkara (48) and Mahela Jayawardene (103 not out) added 62 for the third wicket. Jayawardene became the sixth batsman to hit a century in a World Cup Final. He remains the only batsman to register a hundred in a losing cause in a World Cup Final. Sri Lanka ended with 6 for 274 at 5.48 runs per over.

The Sri Lankans hit back with vengeance, Lasith Malinga (right) had Sehwag lbw for a second ball duck and Tendulkar caught behind for 18. India was on her knees at 2 for 31 with their prolific openers back in the pavilion. This plunged the 40,000 plus spectators to gloom. Game on!

Iron-willed Gambhir (97 off 122 balls with nine fours) and 22 year-old Kohli (35 from 49 balls) steadied the ship adding 83 runs for the third wicket before Kohli fell to a marvellous return catch by Dilshan.

At 3 for 114, it was anyone's game but then came skipper, keeper, hitter and winner MS Dhoni and the mood of the crowd changed from despair to optimism and gradually to ecstasy. He was the dominant partner in partnerships of 109 with Gambhir and had an unbroken 54 run stand with Yuvraj Singh, the Player of the Series.

Dhoni's unbeaten 91 (with eight fours and two sixes) came off 79 balls for a Strike Rate of 115.18.

India totalled 4 for 277 to win the fluctuating Final by 6 wickets with 10 balls in hand. Man of the Match Dhoni had contributed richly by his inspiring innings. It was

# CRICKET WORLD CUP

**2010-11** INDIA
SRI LANKA
BANGLADESH

KERSI MEHER-HOMJI

the highest run-chase ever achieved in a World Cup Final. The victory sparked the most delirious scenes of celebration ever seen on the subcontinent.

India became the first team to win a World Cup Final on home soil.

Playing his sixth and last World Cup match, Tendulkar and coach Gary Kirsten were carried around the outfield cheered lustily by rapturous spectators. Kohli summed up the feelings of all by saying, "He [Tendulkar] has carried the burden of the nation for 21 years. It is time we carried him on our shoulders."

# CRICKET WORLD CUP
## 2014-15 AUSTRALIA & NEW ZEALAND

KERSI MEHER-HOMJI

## On Top Down Under

The 11th World Cup in 2014-15 was dominated by the host nations, Australia and New Zealand. It was literally a case of "on top down under". Both entered the Final which Australia won, watched by 93,013 spectators at the Melbourne Cricket Ground.

Like in the previous World Cup, 14 teams participated in two Pools:

**Pool A:** Australia, England, New Zealand, Sri Lanka, Bangladesh, Afghanistan, Scotland.

**Pool B:** South Africa, West Indies, India, Pakistan, Zimbabwe, Ireland, United Arab Emirates.

New Zealand started her campaign for this World Cup by winning their first six matches. Their biggest satisfaction was beating Australia by one wicket at Auckland. With fast-medium bowler Trent Boult taking 5 for 27, Australia was bowled out for 151 in 32.2 overs.

In reply, New Zealand's opening batsman Brendon McCullum (right) played a captain's innings of 50 at a run rate of over 200. But his dismissal signalled a collapse, Ross Taylor and Grant Elliott were dismissed off successive deliveries from fast bowler Mitchell Starc on either side of the lunch break. New Zealand lost three wickets for one run and was 4 for 79 in the ninth over. Kane Williamson halted the Kiwi slide with his unbeaten 45 off 42 balls.

He carried New Zealand to 131 but the match took a further twist as three wickets tumbled in successive overs and they were 7 for 145, needing seven runs to win. Williamson was batting faultlessly but erred in taking a single from Starc, exposing the tail-enders. Needing six runs to win with only number 11 batsman Boult remaining Williamson hit the first ball from Pat Cummins for a six and the crowd of 40,053 at Eden Park exploded. New Zealand won by one wicket. Despite Williamson's heroics with the bat, Boult was adjudged Man of the Match for dismantling the Australian batting and remaining unbeaten at the end.

Just as players from host countries India, Sri Lanka and Pakistan had dominated the 2010-11 World Cup, Australia and New Zealand cricketers had a lion's share of all the statistical highlights in this World Cup.

New Zealand's Martin Guptill scored most runs, 547 (at an average of 68.37) in nine matches with two centuries.

# CRICKET WORLD CUP
## 2014-15 AUSTRALIA & NEW ZEALAND
### KERSI MEHER-HOMJI

Guptill (right) made the highest individual score, 237 not out against West Indies at Wellington on March 21. This was off 163 balls and included 24 fours and 11 sixes. One of his sixes was the longest, measured at 110 metres.

New Zealand's Brendon McCullum had the highest Strike Rate (SR) of 188.50 when totalling 328 runs at 36.44 in nine matches (minimum qualification: 150 runs). The second highest SR was by Australia's Glenn Maxwell (182.02 while belting 324 runs at 64.80 in eight matches).

Australia's left-arm fast bowler Starc and New Zealand's left-arm fast-medium bowler Boult took most wickets; Starc 22 wickets at an average of 10.18, Boult 22 at 16.86.

Starc's bowling average of 10.18 was the best in this World Cup (minimum qualification: 5 wickets).

Among those who bowled 20 overs or more, Starc had the best economy rate of 3.50 followed by New Zealand's Daniel Vettori (4.04) and Australia's Josh Hazlewood (4.10).

Starc was named Player of the Series in this World Cup.

New Zealand's fast-medium bowler Tim Southee had the best bowling spell, 7 for 33 against England at Wellington. The next best were Starc, 6 for 28 against New Zealand at Auckland, Boult 5 for 27 against Australia at Auckland and Mitchell Marsh 5 for 33 against England at Melbourne.

Australia's Brad Haddin made the most dismissals, 16 (all catches) in eight matches.

Australia made the highest team total, 6 for 417 against Afghanistan at Perth on March 4. Australia won this match by 275 runs. Both are World Cup records.

Not all records had an ANZ alliance.

Sri Lanka's Kumar Sangakkara had the highest batting average of 108.20. He hit four consecutive centuries, becoming the first player to do so in the history of One Day Internationals.

# CRICKET WORLD CUP

## 2014-15  AUSTRALIA & NEW ZEALAND

### KERSI MEHER-HOMJI

Chris Gayle (right) from the West Indies became the first player to hit a double century in the World Cup. His 215 off 147 balls included 16 sixes, another World Cup record. This was against Zimbabwe at Canberra on February 24, 2015. Guptill broke this record 25 days later at Wellington.

The highest partnership was of 372 runs for the second wicket between Gayle and Marlon Samuels in the above match.

England's 1.70 meters tall fast-medium bowler Steven Finn took a hat-trick on the first day of this World Cup, against Australia at Melbourne on February 14. Off-spinner Jean Paul Duminy of South Africa also performed a hat-trick against Sri Lanka in the quarter-final at Sydney on March 18. It was the ninth hat-trick in World Cup history.

This World Cup will be remembered for some thrillers.

**Ireland vs United Arab Emirates (UAE) at Brisbane:** Shaiman Anwar scored a quick 106 for UAE. But with Gary Wilson and Kevin O'Brien (108 runs off 68 balls) scoring freely, Ireland won by two wickets in the final over.

**Afghanistan vs Scotland at Dunedin:** In reply to Scotland's 210, Afghanistan was 7 down for 97. Then Samiullah Sanwari belted five sixes (three in one over) in his 96 and they won by one wicket in the last over.

**New Zealand vs Bangladesh at Hamilton:** Bangladesh totalled 7 for 288, (Mahmudullah 128 not out). New Zealand opener Martin Guptill struck 131. Tim Southee smashed a six and a four in the 49$^{th}$ over and the Kiwis won by three wickets.

As expected, the teams to make the quarter-finals were New Zealand, Australia, Sri Lanka and Bangladesh from Pool A; and South Africa, India, Pakistan and West Indies from Pool B. The highlight of the quarter-final match between South Africa and Sri Lanka was the hat-trick taken by South Africa's Duminy.

Australia, New Zealand, South Africa and India made it to the semi-finals with ease.

The semi-final between New Zealand and South Africa at Auckland was a thriller. In a rain-interrupted match, South Africa made 5 for 281 in 43 overs, Faf du Plessis scoring 82 and AB de Villiers 65 not out. Then came rains and the match

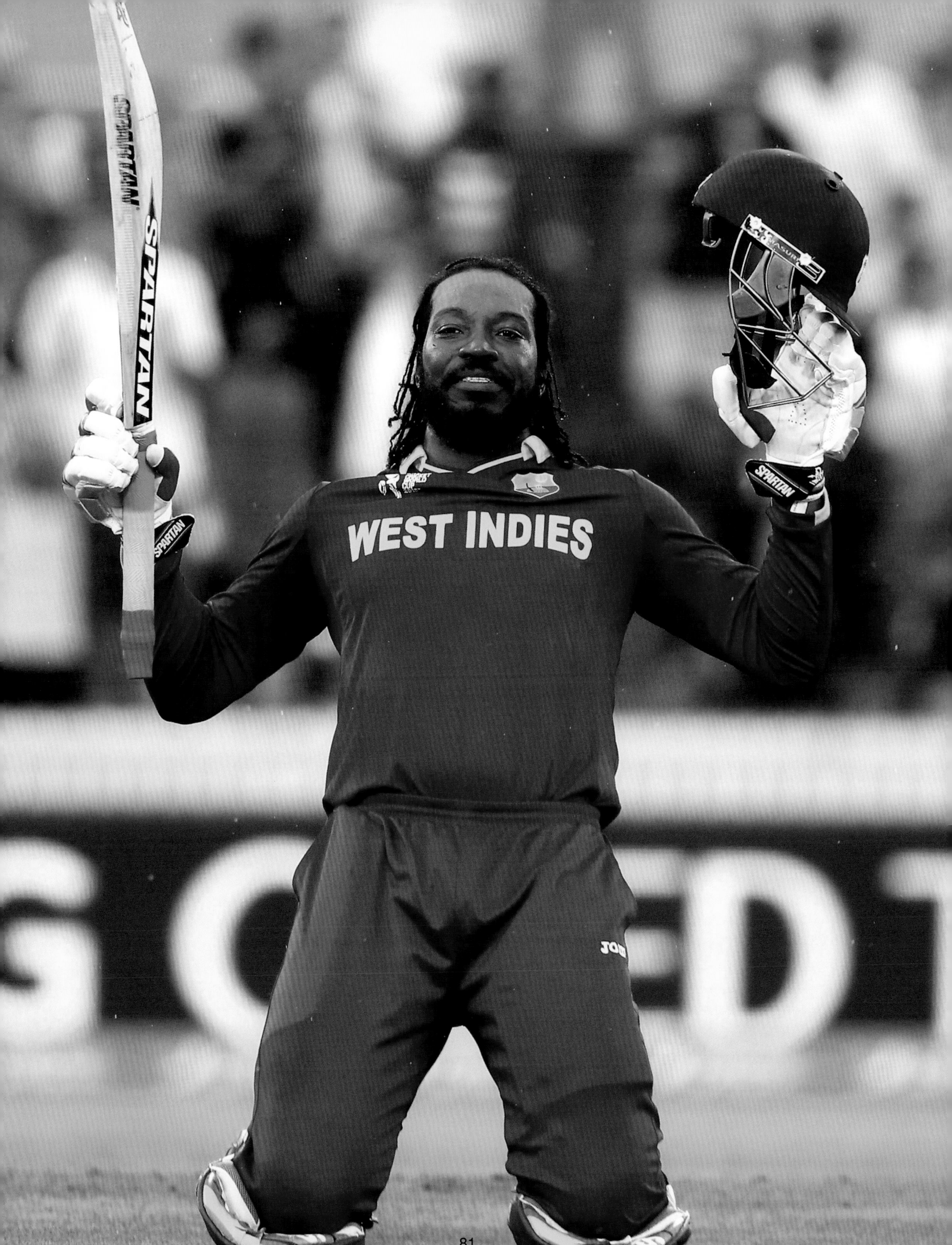
WEST INDIES
SPARTAN

# CRICKET WORLD CUP
## 2014-15 AUSTRALIA & NEW ZEALAND
### KERSI MEHER-HOMJI

was reduced to 43 overs. David Miller smashed 49 off only 18 balls. Corey Anderson took 3 for 72 but proved expensive as he was hit for 12 runs per over.

New Zealand chasing a revised target of 298 runs in 43 overs was given a blistering start by McCullum scoring 59. With 94 runs needed off 70 deliveries, de Villiers squandered a run out chance. Then with only 14 required off seven balls Grant Elliott was about to be caught by substitute fielder Farhaan Berhardien but there was a collision. Duminy was watching the ball in the sky and did not see Berhardien. The two collided and Elliott got a life. Call it a comedy of errors but the Proteas did not see it that way!

Now New Zealand needed 12 runs in the final over for a thrilling climax. Elliott drove the penultimate ball from express fast bowler Dale Steyn over long-on for a six and New Zealand won by four wickets to enter a World Cup Final for the first time.

Skipper McCullum paid tribute to former great New Zealand batsman Martin Crowe by saying, "Martin Crowe has been instrumental in helping the guys within the team."

In the other semi-final at the Sydney Cricket Ground, Australia defeated India, the World Cup holders, by 95 runs to make it to the Final. Opener Aaron Finch (81) and Man of the Match Steve Smith(right) (105) added 182 runs in 31 overs for the second wicket. To Australia's 7 for 328, India replied with 233.

In a lop-sided Final Australia trounced New Zealand by seven wickets at the Melbourne Cricket Ground and won the World Cup. On foreign turf, the Black Caps lost their air of invincibility.

Grant Elliott (83) and Ross Taylor (40) added 111 runs for the fourth wicket for New Zealand but the rest fell to the pace of Mitchell Johnson, James Faulkner and Mitchell Starc and were bowled out for 183 runs in 45 overs.

Australia reached the winning target easily with seven wickets and 101 balls in hand. Smith (56 not out) and skipper Michael Clarke (74) added 112 for the third wicket. Clarke had earlier announced that this would be his last one-day International and received standing ovation from the MCG crowd of over 90,000. What a grand finale to international cricket for 'Pup Clarkey', leaving the scene of his many triumphs on a victory note!

# CRICKET WORLD CUP
## 2014-15 AUSTRALIA & NEW ZEALAND
### KERSI MEHER-HOMJI

Faulkner was made Man of the Final and Starc the Player of the Series.

Australia had won the World Cup for a record fifth time. The next best are the West Indies and India twice each and Pakistan and Sri Lanka once each. Australia has won most matches, 62 (including at one stage, 25 in a row); followed by New Zealand 48, India 46, England and West Indies 41 each, Pakistan 40 and South Africa and Sri Lanka 35 each.

Australia also leads on winning percentage, 75.30%; followed by South Africa (65.45%), India (62.83%), New Zealand (61.53%), West Indies (58.57%), England (58.45%), Pakistan (57.97%) and Sri Lanka (50%).

Will home advantage help England in the 2019 World Cup as it did India and Sri Lanka in 2010-11 and Australia and New Zealand in 2014-15?

# CRICKET WORLD CUP

## Kersi Meher-Homji

## World Cup XIs for top eight teams

Let us now select the strongest World Cup teams (an XI plus a 12th man and three reserves) from each of the eight senior teams; England, Australia, South Africa, the West Indies, New Zealand, India, Pakistan and Sri Lanka.

The criteria for selection are less stringent; minimum 450 runs for batsmen, 15 wickets for bowlers and 15 dismissals (catches plus stumpings) for wicket-keepers. Statistics of the selected players from each country are in the statistical section.

Let us start with **ENGLAND,** the venue of four World Cups (including the first three) and of the 12th one in 2019.

Despite playing in all 11 World Cups, the statistics of individual players from England have been disappointing when compared with players from other major countries.

Graham Gooch will open the batting with Alec Stewart. Apart from scoring 606 runs Stewart also took 21 catches and stumped two batsmen. He will keep wickets for England. Gooch will captain the team, having won five of the eight matches captained for a win percentage of 71.42.

Ian Bell will come in at one wicket down followed by Allan Lamb. We need acceleration in the run-rate and Kevin Pietersen (strike rate 84.06) will provide just that at number five. Graeme Hick will come in next then the great all-rounder Ian 'Biffy' Botham (right).

The team is rich in fast to fast-medium bowlers but impoverished in spinning department. Bob Willis and Jimmy Anderson will open the attack followed by Botham, Andrew Flintoff and Phil DeFreitas. None of the quality spinners has reached our criterion of 15 wickets so part time off-spinner Hick (five wickets at 41.60) will have to be England's sole spinner.

**Here is my World Cup XI from England (in batting order):**

1. Graham Gooch (captain)
2. Alex Stewart (wicket keeper)
3. Ian Bell
4. Allan Lamb
5. Kevin Pietersen
6. Graeme Hick
7. Ian Botham
8. Andrew Flintoff
9. Phil DeFreitas
10. Jimmy Anderson
11. Bob Willis.
**12th Man:** Paul Collingwood.
**Reserves:** Darren Gough, Chris Old and Vic Marks.

# CRICKET WORLD CUP

**Australia**

Dynamic openers Matthew Hayden and Adam Gilchrist (right) will give Australia a flying start. As stated in the previous Chapter, they have been associated in five century partnerships for the first wicket in the World Cup; highest being 172 against Sri Lanka at Bridgetown in 2006-07. Gilchrist will keep wickets, having made 52 dismissals (45 catches and seven stumpings).

Ricky Ponting will come in at number three. Besides his mountain of runs (1743, second only to Sachin Tendulkar from India), he took most catches in the World Cup for a non wicket-keeper, 28.

Between the three, they smashed 73 sixes in 99 matches; Hayden 23 in 22 matches, Gilchrist 19 in 31 and Ponting 31 in 46. They also hit nine centuries; Hayden three, Gilchrist one and Ponting five.

Ponting is my choice as the captain. He captained most times, 29 matches and won most matches 26, for a win percentage of 92.85.

Elegant stroke player Mark Waugh (1004 runs at 52.84) with four centuries comes in next, followed by ambidextrous Michael Clarke who bats right-handed but bowls slow left-arm orthodox.

Never-say-never all-rounder Steve Waugh will bat at number six. Apart from his gritty batting (978 runs at 48.90), he bowls at his best in the death overs getting vital wickets in the thrilling final overs.

Has the run-rate gone down? Then holler for a Symonds, Andrew Symonds. He averaged an incredible 103.00 at a Strike Rate of 93.29, belting 10 sixes. He was also a right arm medium-pace bowler and an off-spinner who fielded brilliantly.

We need two fast bowlers and two spinners (a leg spinner and an off spinner). Who will spearhead the attack? The selection is easy: Express fast bowler Brett Lee and the master swinger Glenn McGrath who took the most number of wickets, 71 with the best bowling figures of 7 for 15 – both are records in the World Cup. Andy Bichel's 7 for 20 is the second best spell in the World Cup after McGrath's. Bichel also averaged 117.00 with the bat scoring 117 runs in three innings, not out twice.

Shane Warne, the living legend, is the obvious choice as the leg-break googly bowler.

Left-arm spinner Brad Hogg is my choice as the other spinner. To quote *ESPNcricinfo*, "With his booming grin, zooming flipper and hard-to-pick wrong'un, Brad Hogg is Australia's most mercurial chinaman bowler since 'Chuck' Fleetwood-Smith in the 1930s."

**Here is my World Cup Australian XI in batting order:**
1. Matthew Hayden 2. Adam Gilchrist (wicket keeper) 3. Ricky Ponting (captain) 4. Mark Waugh 5. Michael Clarke 6. Steve Waugh 7. Andrew Symonds 8. Brett Lee 9. Shane Warne 10. Brad Hogg 11. Glenn McGrath.
**12th man:** Damien Fleming.
**Reserves:** David Boon, Dean Jones and Shane Watson.

# CRICKET WORLD CUP

**South Africa**

Left-handed Graeme Smith will open the innings and captain the team. He won 11 of the 18 matches captained for a win percentage of 64.70. Who will be his opening partner? My choice is the adventurous right-handed Herschelle Gibbs (right) known for his 'six appeal'. Master batsman AB de Villiers will come in at number three. He shares a World Cup record of hitting 37 sixes with Chris Gayle of West Indies.

Next batsmen in will be the renowned all-rounder Jacques Kallis (1148 runs 21 wickets) and the reliable batsman Faf du Plessis. Mark Boucher (381 runs and 31 catches behind the stumps) will keep wickets.

Express fast bowler Dale Steyn will open the attack with Allan Donald. Makhaya Ntini and all-rounder Shaun Pollock will be brought in the attack later on. Imran Tahir will test the opposing batsmen with his leg-break googlies.

**Here is my World Cup South African XI in batting order:**
1. Graeme Smith (captain)
2. Herschelle Gibbs
3. AB de Villiers
4. Jacques Kallis
5. Faf du Plessis
6. Mark Boucher (wicket keeper)
7. Shaun Pollock
8. Dale Steyn
9. Allan Donald
10. Imran Tahir
11. Makhaya Ntini.
**12th man:** Hashim Amla.
**Reserves:** Gary Kirsten, Lance Klusener and Morne Morkel.

# CRICKET WORLD CUP

**The West Indies**

The Windies have three top-line openers, the established pair of Gordon Greenidge and Desmond Haynes as also the limited-overs specialist six hitter Gayle (right). After a lot of deliberation I have gone for Greenidge and Gayle to open with Haynes coming in at number three. Gayle's 16 sixes in his knock of 215 against Zimbabwe at Canberra on February 24, 2015 is a record in the World Cup.

Next ones in will be the acknowledged master blasters Viv Richards and Brian Lara. Clive Lloyd will captain the side, having won 15 of the 17 matches he captained for a win percentage of 88.23. This trio is recognised as the greatest annihilators of bowlers fast or spin. Between them they hit 42 sixes.

Jeff Dujon (112 runs and 19 catches behind the stumps and one stumping) will keep wickets and bat at number seven. To quote Mike Selvey on Jeff Dujon from *ESPNcricinfo*: "It was one of the most spectacular sights of cricket in the 1980s. A great West Indian fast bowler - any of several suspects - roared on by a partisan Caribbean crowd, a short ball rearing, the batsman fending and edging, and behind the stumps, a lithe athlete leaping and plunging to take another one-handed blinder. Jeff Dujon was the gymnastic hub of those all-conquering Windies sides, a man who never participated in a losing series and whose tally of victims [in Test cricket] has been exceeded only by Ian Healy and Rod Marsh."

We need four bowlers and we have five of the most feared express fast bowlers in Curtly Ambrose, Andy Roberts, Michael Holding, Malcolm Marshall and Courtney Walsh. Two of them have to be excluded as we need a spinner.

Of the five, Ambrose, Holding and Walsh have better figures so out go Roberts and Marshall.

The best bowling spell for a West Indian is by quickie Winston Davis who took 7 for 51 against Australia at Headingley in the 1983 World Cup. Remarkably, it was his debut in the World Cup. But due to the presence of many lightening fast bowlers there is no room for him.
Who will be the spinner for the team? Of the two off-spinners, Roger Harper has better figures than Carl Hooper. Being a sharp fielder, having taken 13 catches, Hooper will be the 12th man.

**Here is my World Cup West Indies XI in batting order:**
1. Gordon Greenidge 2. Chris Gayle 3. Desmond Haynes 4. Viv Richards 5. Brian Lara
6. Clive Lloyd (captain) 7. Jeff Dujon (wicket keeper) 8. Roger Harper 9. Michael Holding 10. Courtney Walsh
11. Curtly Ambrose.
**12th man:** Carl Hooper.
**Reserves:** Andy Roberts, Shivnarine Chanderpaul and Richie Richardson.

# CRICKET WORLD CUP

**New Zealand**

Glenn Turner and Stephen Fleming will open the innings. Having won 16 of the 27 matches for a win percentage of 61.53, Fleming will be the skipper.

The elegant and prolific batsman Martin Crowe (right) will bat at number three. He was adjudged Player of the Series in the World Cup 1991-92 in Australasia by scoring 456 runs at a Bradman-like batting average of 114.00 (his run aggregate being the highest by any batsman in this World Cup) and for his innovative captaincy. In the opening match at Auckland he shocked the 1987 World Cup champions Australia by beating them by 37 runs on February 2, 1992. He scored an unbeaten 100 and disoriented the Aussies by giving the new ball to off-spinner Dipak Patel.

Martin Guptill whose unbeaten 237 against the West Indies at Wellington on March 21, 2015 is a record for an individual innings in the World Cup will come in at number 4.

Scott Styris who had an outstanding 2006-07 season scoring 499 runs at 83.16 comes in next followed by Ross Taylor. Run rate slowing down? We need a hitter now. So come in wicket keeper batsman Brendon McCullum, the batsman who skied 29 sixes and had a strike rate of 120.84. He also made 34 dismissals behind the stumps.

Now to the attack. Is Sir Richard Hadlee, New Zealand's greatest cricketer and one of the greatest all-rounders in the history of the game, a certainty? Not so. Statistically, he has been pushed aside by fast and furious Shane Bond and accurate seamer Tim Southee. Hadlee did not fire as a batsman, only 149 runs in 13 matches at a disappointing average of 16.55 to complement his 22 wickets at 19.13.

All-rounder Chris Harris, left hand bat and right arm medium pacer, will be the first change bowler. Slow left-arm orthodox Daniel Vettori will be the sole spinner.

**Here is my World Cup New Zealand XI in batting order:**
1. Glenn Turner
2. Stephen Fleming (captain)
3. Martin Crowe
4. Martin Guptill
5. Scott Styris
6. Ross Taylor
7. Brendon McCullum (wicket keeper)
8. Chris Harris
9. Daniel Vettori
10. Tim Southee
11. Shane Bond.
**12th man:** Chris Cairns.
**Reserves:** Richard Hadlee, Jacob Oram and Trent Boult.

# CRICKET WORLD CUP

**India**

Cricket legend Sachin Tendulkar and daredevil Virender Sehwag will open the batting. Tendulkar scored 2278 runs at 56.95, highest score 152, strike rate of 88.98, hitting six centuries, 15 fifties, 241 fours and 27 sixes. His run aggregate, number of centuries, fifties and fours hit are World Cup records.

An attacking batsman Sehwag's strike rate was a thundering 106.17 (right).

Just like Richard Hadlee missed out selection in the New Zealand XI, one of the greatest ever Test opening batsmen Sunil Gavaskar (561 runs at 35.06 in 19 World Cup matches) could not be included.

Rahul Dravid, Virat Kohli and Sourav Ganguly come in at numbers 3, 4 and 5. Then walks in all-rounder Kapil Dev at number 6 and wicket-keeper batsman MS Dhoni at number 7.  Kapil Dev scored 669 runs at a strike rate of 115.14 and a top score of 175 not out. He also took 28 wickets at an economy rate of 3.76. Besides scoring 507 runs at a strike rate of 91.18 Dhoni caught 27 and stumped five batsmen.

With so much batting talent the elegant Mohammad Azharuddin could not make the XI.

Zaheer Khan will open India's attack with Kapil Dev. Javagal Srinath will be the first change. Leg-break googly bowler Anil Kumble and off-spinner Ravichandran Ashwin will try to spin out the opponents.

It is disappointing that on basis of statistical qualification (minimum 15 wickets), none of the famous spin quartet – Bishan Bedi, EAS Prasanna, BS Chandrasekhar, Srini Venkataraghavan – had to be excluded. Harbhajan Singh took 20 wickets in 21 matches at a poor average of 40.40, best bowling 3 for 53 and therefore is not included.

It is hard to leave out the mighty left-handed high hitter Yuvraj Singh in the Indian XI. In a World Twenty20 win for India against England at Durban on September 19, 2007, he struck England's Stuart Broad for six sixes in an over. He will be the 12th man for India.

Among Indian bowlers, left-arm medium fast Ashish Nehra had the best bowling figures, 6 for 23 against England at Durban on February 26, 2003.

Who will captain India, Kapil or Dhoni? Kapil led India to her first World Cup victory at Lord's against the mighty Windies in 1983. And skipper Dhoni hit a six in the Final against Sri Lanka at Mumbai to enable India to lift the World Cup in 2010-11.

Kapil won 11 out of 15 matches captained for a win percentage of 73.33. Dhoni won 14 out of 17 matches captained for a win percentage of 85.29. My vote goes for Dhoni.

**Here is my World Cup India XI in batting order:**

1. Sachin Tendulkar 2. Virender Sehwag 3. Rahul Dravid 4. Virat Kohli 5. Sourav Ganguly
6. Kapil Dev 7. MS Dhoni (captain, wicket keeper) 8. Ravichandran Ashwin 9. Anil Kumble
10. Javagal Srinath 11. Zaheer Khan.
**12th man:** Yuvraj Singh.
**Reserves:** Mohammad Azharuddin, Sunil Gavaskar and Ashish Nehra.

# CRICKET WORLD CUP

**Pakistan**

Heavily bearded Saeed Anwar with majestic timing and combative left-handed batsman Aamer Sohail will open the batting for Pakistan. Misbah-ul-Haq will come in at number 3 followed by Javed Miandad, one of the greatest batsmen Pakistan has produced. 'Mr Elegance' Zaheer Abbas (right) will bat at number five.

Then in comes skipper Imran Khan, one of the greatest all-rounders in the history of the game. He scored 666 runs at 35.05 and took 34 wickets at 19.26. Having won 14 out of 22 matches, he had the win percentage of 63.63. He also led Pakistan to her only World Cup win in 1991-92.

Kamran Akmal, (249 runs at 27.66, highest score 55, taking 11 catches and stumping six batsmen) will keep the wickets.

Wasim Akram (55 wickets at 23.83, best bowling 5 for 28) will open the attack with Shoaib Akhtar, one of the fastest bowlers in the history of cricket. Imran will bowl as the first change giving batsmen no chance to settle down. Saqlain Mushtaq will be the off-spinner, arguably the first bowler to master the "doosra". Then Abdul Qadir will confound batsmen with his leg-break googlies.

Shahid Afridi, the unique all-rounder with two googlies, will carry drinks.

**Here is my World Cup Pakistan XI in batting order:**

1. Saeed Anwar
2. Aamer Sohail
3. Misbah-ul-Haq
4. Javed Miandad
5. Zaheer Abbas
6. Imran Khan (captain)
7. Kamran Akmal (wicket keeper)
8. Wasim Akram
9. Shoaib Akhtar
10. Saqlain Mushtaq
11. Abdul Qadir.
**12th man:** Shahid Afridi.
**Reserves:** Waqar Younis, Rameez Raja and Ijaz Ahmed.

# CRICKET WORLD CUP

**Sri Lanka**

World-class left-hander Sanath Jayasuriya (right)was a useful all-rounder for Sri Lanka. He was a handy left-arm orthodox bowler. His dare devil batting as an opener was the inspiration behind Sri Lanka's World Cup win in 1995-96. He will open the batting with the aggressive stroke player Tillakaratne Dilshan.

Elegant batsman Mahela Jayawardene comes in at number 3.

Short in height standing at 5'3½" but tall in achievements Aravinda de Silva was a delight to watch, being an entertaining and attacking batsman. His finest hour was scoring a match-winning and unbeaten 107 in the 1995-96 World Cup Final at Lahore. It was Sri Lanka's finest hour too winning their first and only World Cup. Sri Lanka recovered from 2 for 23 to beat reigning champion Australia by seven wickets. He received Man of the Match award from Pakistan's Prime Minister Benazir Bhutto.

Sri Lanka's wicket-keeper batsman Kumar Sangakkara comes in at number five. Besides scoring 1532 runs with five centuries he also made the most dismissals, 54 (41 caught and 13 stumped) in the history of the World Cup. Stockily built left-handed batsman Arjuna Ranatunga will captain the team and bat at number six. He had captained Sri Lanka in winning their only World Cup at Lahore on March 17, 1996. Under him Sri Lanka won eight of the 11 matches played for a win percentage of 72.72.

Next man in will be current batsman Upul Tharanga followed by the dashing Roshan Mahanama.

Fast medium Chaminda Vaas will open the attack. Sri Lanka's hairy, fiery fast-medium bowler Lasith Malinga will partner him using the new ball. As already mentioned, he is the only bowler to take two hat-tricks in the World Cup which include the unique achievement of taking four wickets in four balls.

The controversial off-spinner Muttiah Muralitharan (right) is a certainty. In 40 matches he pocketed 68 wickets at 19.63. His partner in spin will be opening batsman Jayasuriya, a slow left arm spinner.

**Here is my World Cup Sri Lanka XI in batting order:**
1.Sanath Jayasuriya 2. Tillakaratne Dilshan 3. Mahela Jayawardene 4. Aravinda de Silva
5. Kumar Sangakkara (wicket keeper) 6. Arjuna Ranatunga (captain) 7. Upul Tharanga
8. Roshan Mahanama 9. Chaminda Vaas 10. Lasith Malinga 11. Muttiah Muralitharan.
**12th man:** Marvan Atapattu.
**Reserves:** Asanka Gurusinha, Ashantha de Mel and Pramodya Wickremasinghe.

In conclusion let me state that I do not expect critics and readers to agree with my selections of the best World Cup XIs (plus 12th man and reserves) from each of the eight major countries. Although based mainly on statistics, in some grey areas personal choice has come in to play.

Who will win the mythical World Cup from the eight teams selected above? I reckon that the West Indies, Australia, Sri Lanka and India (or South Africa) will make the semi final. The Final could be fought out between the West Indies and Australia – like in the inaugural 1975 World Cup.

This will not be the scenario for the real 2019 World Cup.

# CRICKET WORLD CUP

# Classic Cliff-Hangers

Kersi Meher-Homji

**Tail-enders behind Windies' one wicket win**
**(Pakistan vs West Indies at Birmingham, 1975)**

The first three World Cups, in 1975, 1979 and 1983, were called The Prudential Cup and were of 60 overs duration. The first nail-biting match was fought out between Pakistan and the West Indies on June 11, 1975 which the latter won by one wicket in the final pulsating over. This thriller hung in balance till the very end. With skipper Majid Khan, Mushtaq Mohammed and Wasim Raja scoring fifties Pakistan totalled 7 for 266 in 60 overs.

The ultimate champions West Indies were in trouble at 5 for 99 and 9 for 203, despite captain Clive Lloyd's 53 as Pakistan's fast medium bowler and ultimate Man of the Match Sarfraz Nawaz claimed four victims. Lloyd was upset when given out caught behind off teenager Javed Miandad.

But number 8 batsman Deryck Murray (61 not out) and no. 11 Andy Roberts (24 not out) showed determination adding 64 precious runs for the unbroken last wicket and the West Indies won by one wicket with only two balls remaining.

The ground was invaded by the Windies supporters swamping the unbeaten heroes Murray and Roberts.

## When Australia ran out of luck – literally
## (Australia vs West Indies, Final at Lord's, 1975)

The two strongest teams, West Indies and Australia, entered the Final of the inaugural World Cup and there were more expatriate West Indians than local Englishmen in the Stands, judging from the cacophonic sounds of bugles and bongo drums.

Prior to the match the Aussies were relaxed but the Windies were tense. Ian Chappell won the toss and sent the Windies in to bat. Opener Roy Fredericks hooked a Dennis Lillee bouncer over the boundary but lost balance and fell on his wicket. You may call it "six and out"!

At 3 for 50, captain Clive Lloyd joined Rohan Kanhai. The bespactacled skipper was at his blistering best, savaging Lillee, Jeff Thomson and Gary Gilmour. He reached his century off just 82 balls as he smashed 12 fours and two sixes. The normally attacking Kanhai watched as his captain ran riot blasting102 in 108 minutes. Gilmour (5 for 48) dismissed both and the Windies totalled 8 for 291 in 60 overs.

Australia replied strongly being 1 for 81 at one stage but Alan Turner, Ian Chappell and Greg Chappell were run out by Viv Richards. Calm and cool, Doug Walters scored 35. When the ninth wicket fell at 233 Australia needed 59 runs for victory in 7.1 overs with only tail-enders Thomson and Lillee remaining. It seemed all over but the Aussie speedsters 'Lilian Thomson' turned into debonair hitters. Now it came down to this: 21 needed in the final two overs.

Vanburn Holder bowled a no-ball, Thomson skied it and Fredericks 'caught' it. In the pandemonium, the crowd did not hear the no-ball call and believing that the Windies had won, thousands swarmed onto the pitch, bongo drums and all. The fielders were knocked about and the ball was lost as Lillee and Thomson kept running. The umpires called it a dead ball and three runs were added. But the break ruined Thomson's concentration and he was the fifth Aussie to get run out and Australia lost by 17 runs at 8.43 p.m.

## It was touch and go but England enter the Final – only just
## (England vs New Zealand, semi-final at Manchester, 1979)

England was engaged in two thrillers within four days and won both times. After beating Pakistan by 14 runs at Leeds, they met a confident New Zealand in the semi-final at Manchester.

Sent in to bat, England made 8 for 221 in 60 overs, skipper and opener Mike Brearley a steady 53, Graham Gooch a confident 71 and Derek Randall an unbeaten 42. Fiery fast New Zealand bowler Richard Hadlee tied down his opponents.

One six from Gooch remains memorable. It soared towards and through the sightscreen, leaving a hole on the ground which remained unmended for many years. The Kiwis were given a good start by skipper John Wright (69) and Bruce Edgar but the pace bowling of Michael Hendrick and electrifying fielding by Randall restricted their run chase.

It was touch and go as they needed 43 runs from five overs. There was drama when Warren Lees hit Hendrick hard and high to mid-on. Geoff Boycott got under the ball and "caught" it. However, his feet touched the boundary rope and it was signaled as a six!

In the final over 14 runs were required but England's master all-rounder Ian Botham conceded only four runs and England won by nine runs to enter their first World Cup final which they lost to the mighty Windies by 92 runs at Lord's.

Gooch's aggressive innings earned him the second man of the Match award within a fortnight.

## The Kiwis get their revenge over England
## (England vs New Zealand at Birmingham, 1983)

The 1983 World Cup was full of surprises, little fancied Zimbabwe beating star-studded Australians (including Allan Border, Rod Marsh, Dennis Lillee and Jeff Thomson) by 13 runs and almost defeating India (but for Kapil Dev's magnificent century after India was reeling at 5 for 17), India beating the champions West Indies in an earlier match and later in the Final.

Now to the England - New Zealand revenge match. England made a confident start with Graeme 'Foxy' Fowler hitting 69 and David Gower an unbeaten 92 off 96 balls. The Kiwi bowlers Richard Hadlee, Lance Cairns, Jeremy Coney and Ewen Chatfield hit back and England lost their last three wickets for one run to be dismissed for 234 runs in 55.2 overs.

Fast bowler Bob Willis dismissed the New Zealand openers for three runs. Thus between the two teams, five wickets had fallen for four runs. Cometh the hour and cometh the men as captain Geoff Howarth (60 run out) and Man of the Match Coney (66 not out) led their team to a two wicket win with only one ball remaining.

It was a day to rue for tall England skipper Willis whose fine figures of 12-1-42-4 went unrewarded. Worse was to come for England. Their chairman of selectors and former great batsman Peter May described them as "arrogant" and "indisciplined".

In the Final, India – quoted at 66 to 1 before the Cup commenced – defeated firm favorites West Indies by 43 runs at Lord's. The match was not so much a cliff-hanger as a shock from a live wire to an extinguishing flame.

## It was Kapil against the World
## (India vs West Indies at Lord's, 1983)

No one had anticipated India to win the World Cup in 1983 after their disappointing shows in 1975 and 1979. Their climb to the top had more snakes than ladders. They beat top teams West Indies and Australia in the earlier rounds but almost lost to lowly Zimbabwe.

Overconfident India was down 5 for 17 and 7 for 78 against Zimbabwe but was rescued by skipper Kapil Dev (175 not out with 6 sixes and 16 fours), scored 8 for 266 in 60 overs and went on to win by 31 runs.

Now to the epic Final at Lord's. Their opponents were the mighty Windies who had won both the previous World Cups in 1975 and 1979. Sent in to bat, India was dismissed for 183 and the writing was on the wall. The sports editors of some dailies must have planned their headlines in advance: "Windies perform the hat-trick of World Cup wins".

It didn't go according to the script. The master blaster Viv Richards scored a quick 33 with seven fours but Kapil took an incredible catch on the boundary line to send him back. From then on, it was climb down for the Windies and India shocked the world by winning by 43 runs and lifting their first World Cup.

Mohinder Amarnath was adjudged the Man of the Match after scoring 26 runs and taking 3 for 12 off seven accurate overs. But it was Madan Lal who had made early breakthroughs dismissing Desmond Haynes, Viv Richards and Larry Gomes and had figures of 3-31.

The victorious Indian team danced and sang all night at their hotel. The next day, 26th June became a public holiday in India.

## How a tour manager won a thriller
## (Australia vs India at Chennai, 1987-88)

Renamed the Reliance Cup, World Cup 1987-88 was played outside UK for the first time and was comprised of 50-over matches. It was also rich in cliff-hangers.

Australian cricket was in the doldrums in mid-1980s after the simultaneous retirements of Greg Chappell, Dennis Lillee and Rod Marsh and loss of key players due to their South African connections. No one expected Australia to enter the semi-final, let alone lift the1987-88 World Cup.

This changed after their first match against India at Chennai. Australia scored 6 for 268 after Geoff Marsh (110 off 141 balls and including one six and seven fours) and David Boon (49) put on 110 runs for the opening wicket at almost 5 runs per over.  The alert Australian manager Alan Crompton had noticed that a hit from Dean Jones signaled as a four was actually a six. At lunch Crompton, the umpires and captains Allan Border and Kapil Dev watched the video and two runs were added to the total. The win target now became 271.

India started her reply confidently and was 2 for 207 with sparkling batting from Sunil Gavaskar, Kris Srikkanth and Navjot Sidhu. Gavaskar's strokeplay delighted columnist Henry Blofeld who described his back foot drive off Craig McDermott as "the stroke of the year". When Gavaskar hit off-spinner Peter Taylor for a four and a six, the huge crowd of nearly 40,000 erupted in joy.

But in a devastating second spell, fast bowler McDermott took four wickets. In the last over India needed six runs for a win with the last man Maninder Singh on strike.

"Ice-man" Steve Waugh conceded two runs from his first two deliveries but sent the bearded Maninder's off-stump cart-wheeling out of the ground off the fifth ball and Australia won by one run. This stunned the capacity crowd into silence but the Australian players were in raptures, celebrating as if they had won the World Cup.

For his century, Marsh was adjudged Man of the Match but many said tongue-in-cheek that manager Crompton was the real hero.

This thriller was played a little over one year after the famous tied Test; same opponents, same venue, almost same result.

## Lamb not to the slaughter as England wins by a whisker
## (England vs West Indies at Gujranwala, 1987-88)

Another fluctuating match and the result in doubt till the final pulsating over.

Sent in to bat the West Indies made 7 for 243, Richie Richardson (53 runs) and Jeff Dujon (46) adding 83 runs for the fifth wicket. Then Gus Logie scored 49. England's medium-pacer Neil Foster was the most effective bowler taking 3 for 53.

Opener Graham Gooch made 47 runs but wickets toppled at the other end against the off-spin of Carl Hooper. Then Allan Lamb played a cavalier knock of 67 not out with five fours and a six.

England needed 91 runs to win in the last 10 overs with Lamb the only recognised batsman left. The target remained just as daunting with 34 required in the last four overs. Cool and calm, Lamb collected 15 runs from over no. 48 bowled by speedster Courtney Walsh. Another quickie Patrick Patterson conceded only five runs in the 49th over.

It came down to this, 14 runs needed from the last over. Man of the Match Lamb hit fours off the first two balls from Walsh. Then there were four wides off the third ball followed by a single off a no ball before Neil Foster hit the winning four as England won by two wickets.

The Windies badly missed their express bowlers Malcolm Marshall and Garner – especially at the end. Walsh who had conceded 29 runs from his last nine balls was distraught and devastated.

Man of the Match Lamb said after the narrow win, "It was absolutely boiling in the middle. When we came off I was completely dehydrated and had to replenish with a lot of liquids. Once back in the dressing room I just sat in the bathroom and they kept pouring cold water over me."

## New Zealand wins a chiller despite Houghton's high sixes
## (New Zealand vs Zimbabwe at Hyderabad, 1987-88)

The 1987-88 World Cup was only two days old and three cliff hangers had already been contested .

New Zealand's top three batsmen played confidently and the score was 1 for 143, Martin Snedden (64 runs) adding 59 runs with John Wright (17) for the first wicket and 84 for the second wicket with Martin Crowe (72). But they could not keep up the tempo and made 7 for 242.

Zimbabwe appeared all but gone at 7 for 104. Just then number 9 bat Iain 'Butchy' Butchart joined wicket-keeper batsman Dave Houghton and there was a tsunami of runs as they doubled the score and more. Houghton hit a magnificent 142 off 137 balls, a strike rate of 103.64, smashing 13 fours and six sixes.

He added 117 with Butchart (54 run out) for the eighth wicket before being caught spectacularly by Martin Crowe. This catch was hailed as the catch of this World Cup.

In a climax watched by about 34,000, Zimbabwe needed six runs in the final over but left arm spinner Stephen Boock (pronounced Bock) conceded only two and New Zealand won by three runs with two balls remaining. Snedden said of his opponent Houghton's scintillating innings, "It was an absolute bolt from the blue for me."

Man of the Match Houghton recalled his partner's huge six tongue-in-cheek, "Butchart had hit one straight out of Hyderabad, and I don't know what the next city is, but it landed quite close to it!"

What was the inspiration behind the avalanche of fours and sixes? Houghton explained that he was perspiring profusely losing many kilograms in weight, could not drink water nor could he run, so he smacked fours and sixes instead. Simple!

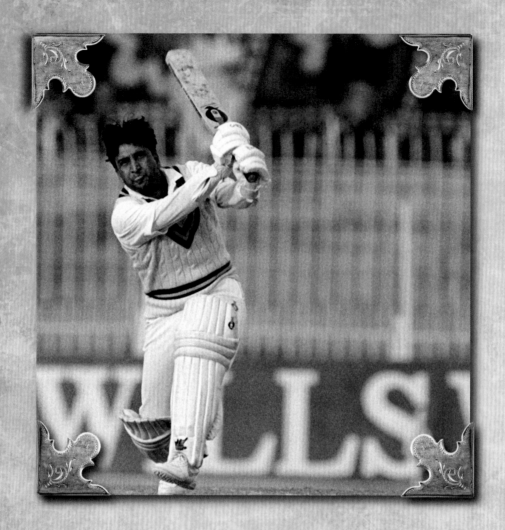

## Qadir's six in the final over gives Pakistan one wicket last ball win
## (Pakistan vs West Indies at Lahore, 1987-88)

The match was in suspense till the final delivery. The West Indies started well with a 91 run opening partnership between Desmond Haynes and debutant Phil Simmons. The latter scored 50 runs off 57 balls hitting eight fours.

Skipper and master blaster Viv Richards hit 51. Opposing captain Imran Khan took 4 for 37 and Wasim Akram 2 for 45 to restrict the Windies to 216 off 49.3 overs.

For Pakistan Rameez Raja and Javed Miandad added 64 for the third wicket. Salim Yousuf was lucky to survive three chances off three balls off medium pacer Eldine Baptiste and went on to top score in the match with 56 off 49 balls, hitting seven fours. With Imran he added 73 runs for the sixth wicket.

In the 49th over, fast bowler Patrick Patterson conceded only two runs and dismissed Wasim Akram. Then Tauseef Ahmed was run out. Now to the electrifying final over from Courtney Walsh; West Indies needing one wicket, Pakistan 14 runs from tail-enders Abdul Qadir and Salim Jaffer.

Walsh conceded 1, 1, 2, 6, 2 and 2 runs and Pakistan won off the last ball by one wicket and a huge crowd in Lahore – almost 50,000 – was in raptures. Thirteen of the 14 runs were hit by Qadir including the fourth ball six and the winning run.

Off the last ball Walsh could have run out Jaffer for backing up too soon and win the game for West Indies but did not.

## Steve Waugh's death-over results in another nail-biting win for Aussies (Australia vs New Zealand at Indore, 1987-88)

In a rain affected match, Australia defeated New Zealand by three runs off the last ball.

It had poured buckets and New Zealand management wanted the match to be abandoned but it went on. Winning the toss, New Zealand captain Jeff Crowe had no hesitation in sending Australia in to bat. Man of the Match David Boon (87 runs off 96 balls) and Dean Jones (52) added 117 runs for the second wicket off 98 balls and Australia smacked 4 for 199 in 30 overs.

NZ took up the challenge, John Wright and the classy batsman Martin Crowe inching towards victory. Then came the sensational last over with New Zealand needing only seven runs with four wickets in hand. Easy?

Not quite. The final over was bowled by guess who? The ice-man Steve Waugh! Like against India ten days earlier he worked another miracle. Off the first ball he dismissed the well set Martin Crowe, caught behind for 58. The next ball he clean-bowled Ian Smith. He allowed only three singles and ran out Martin Snedden off the last ball. NZ ended at 9 for196 to lose by three runs. What a heart-stopper!

There were two more heart-stoppers as England beat West Indies by two wickets and Pakistan defeated West Indies by one wicket.

## Oh Kolkata, it's World Cup for the Aussies
## (Australia vs England at Kolkata, 1987-88)

The above wins against India and New Zealand were just the catalyst Allan Border's men needed. The little-fancied Australians not only entered the semi-final but also beat the Cup favourites Pakistan in Pakistan to make it to the Final. With adrenalin pumping through their veins, they arrived in Kolkata feeling ten feet tall. A bonus for the Aussies was that a majority of the 70,000 plus mostly Indian spectators barracked for them perhaps because they had humiliated arch rival Pakistan.

With Man of the Match David Boon scoring 75 and Mike Veletta an unbeaten 45 Australia totalled 253. They appeared confident as no team till then had scored 254 to win a World Cup.

England started well and at 4 for 188 was on target. But Mike Gatting handed back the initiative when he attempted a reverse sweep off Border and was caught behind.

Now England needed 46 from five overs with five wickets in hand. Steve Waugh bowled a well-set Allan Lamb in the 47th over. Phil DeFreitas gave England hope with 14 runs (4, 6, 4) in McDermott's penultimate over but Waugh had him caught and conceded just 2 runs in the 49th over. England needed 17 runs in the final over but McDermott allowed only nine and Australia won by seven runs to win their first World Cup.

Simon O'Donnell was the unsung hero as he fielded and bowled all 10 overs despite being ill. He was diagnosed with a lymphatic tumour soon after returning home. Happily, he recovered completely.

The Aussies celebrated winning their first World Cup proudly displaying their Trophy on a lap of honour. The huge crowd at Eden Gardens, Kolkata, enjoyed the fantastic fireworks display.

## Long arm of Botham behind England's narrow win
## (England vs India at Perth, 1991-92)

The Benson and Hedges World Cup 1991-92 in Australia and New Zealand was the first to be played in colour clothing and a white ball with some matches played under light.

In the opening match England scored 9 for 236 after skipper Graham Gooch (51 runs) and Robin Smith (91 off 108 balls and including two sixes) added 110 for the second wicket. Then wickets toppled to India's medium-pacers, at one stage England lost six for 27 to go from 3 for 197 to 9 for 224.

India's contrasting openers, sedate Ravi Shastri (only two fours in his 51) and aggressive Kris Srikkanth (39 with seven fours) put on 63 runs. Shastri spooned a tall catch to Phil DeFreitas who dropped it but threw down the stumps.

In an accurate spell Botham dismissed a well set Sachin Tendulkar (35) and Vinod Kambli. Now India needed 51 from seven overs. Soon it became 36 from three overs when last man Javagal Srinath joined Subroto Banerjee. The pair added 26 valiant runs, Banerjee hitting a four and a six – much to the annoyance of the Barmy Army.

But India's march to an unexpected victory (11 runs from the last over) was obstructed by the long and accurate arm of Botham who ran out Srinath, with India nine runs short and four balls remaining. India's captain Mohammad Azharuddin lamented 13 wides bowled by his bowlers.

Earlier Botham had failed with the bat but took 2 for 27 in 10 overs, fielded brilliantly and was adjudged Man of the Match.

## Australia beat India by one run due to an unfair rain rule
## (Australia vs India at Brisbane, 1991-92)

Australia's narrow win was a subject of much debate. The rain rule then was faulty and India was at a disadvantage.

Man of the Match Dean Jones scored a fluent 90 off 108 balls and Australia made 9 for 237 in 50 overs, His second scoring shot was a six off fast-medium bowler Javagal Srinath. India's opening bowlers Kapil Dev and Manoj Prabhakar had identical figures of 3 for 41 each.

Rain stopped play when India was 1 for 45 in the 17th over. Rain cut 15 minutes and three overs from India's innings but the win target was dropped by only two runs; 236 instead of 238.

India attacked with vengeance; skipper Mohammad Azharuddin stroking 93 from 103 balls and Sanjay Manjrekar 47 from 42 balls before both were run out. India needed 13 runs from the last over from tall Tom Moody.

Kiran More hit the first two balls for fours but was bowled off the fourth. Prabhakar took a single but was run out off the fifth delivery. Now India needed four runs off the last ball.

Javagal Srinath lifted the ball high in the sky, Steve Waugh dropped the ball just inside the boundary but threw it accurately to acting wicket-keeper David Boon and last man Venkatapathy Raju was run out. India was all out for 234 to lose by one run.

Thus India had scored three fewer runs in three fewer overs and lost. Illogical, if you ask me.

## Unlikely contestants play a memorable Final
## (England vs Pakistan at Melbourne, 1991-92)

If anyone had suggested a fortnight earlier that Pakistan and England would contest the Final he would have been mocked. Pakistan had lost four of their first five matches and England had lost embarrassingly to Zimbabwe by nine runs. Also England was lucky to beat South Africa in the semi-final because of the ridiculous rain rule which was in play.

Watched by nearly 90,000 at the MCG, the Final was spectacular. Pakistan lost their first two wickets for 24 to the swinging quickie Derek Pringle before flamboyant skipper Imran Khan (72 runs) and Javed Miandad (58) – the sole survivors of World Cup 1975 – added 139 for the third wicket. Then Inzamam-ul-Haq and Wasim Akram put on valuable runs at the end and Pakistan made 6 for 249.

England also lost early wickets cheaply, being 4 for 69 when Neil Fairbrother and Allan Lamb added 72 runs. Man of the Match Wasim Akram (3 for 49) took vital wickets. Imran dismissed the last man Richard Illingworth, enabling Pakistan to win by 22 runs. After the final, the sky was filled with fireworks.

Pakistan had lifted their first and only World Cup. Imran pledged the proceeds of his earnings to the cancer hospital planned in memory of his mother.

The colourful and inspiring Imran Khan who became Pakistan's Prime Minister 26 years later in 2018, said after the 1992 Pakistan triumph, "It was the most fulfilling and satisfying cricket moment of my life."

## Mark Waugh scintillates and Australia wins narrowly
## (Australia vs India at Mumbai, 1995-96)

The World Cup was named The Wills World Cup in 1995-96.

This thriller was the first day-night international in Mumbai and was illuminated by two Australian Marks batting brilliantly; Mark Waugh (126) and Mark Taylor (59). They added 103 runs for the first wicket and Australia totalled 258.

Man of the Match Mark Waugh became the first batsman to score centuries in consecutive World Cup matches, having hit the Kenyan attack for 130 four days previously. Surprisingly Taylor was the more aggressive of the two Marks, hitting Javagal Srinath for a six.

Venkatapathy Raju, his name more difficult to pronounce than his deliveries to decipher by the Aussies, had Taylor caught by Srinath at long-on. Out of Taylor's shadow, Mark Waugh started dominating. He reached his 50 by sweeping Raju for a six.

But they lost their last seven wickets for measly 23 runs including last three wickets for zilch in the last five overs to be all out for 258.

India lost 2 for 7 but recovered through Sachin Tendulkar scoring an explosive 90 (in 84 balls with 14 fours and a six) as the crowd at the Wankhede Stadium in Mumbai chanted "Sachin, Sachin, Sachin!" He went from 12 to 56 in 25 heart-lifting deliveries.

He added 73 runs with the more sedate Sanjay Manjrekar (62). As Indian flags were waving, Mark Waugh had Tendulkar stumped by Ian Healy.

Speedster Damien Fleming claimed 5 for 36 and India fell 16 runs short.

## Miracle at Mohali
## (Australia vs West Indies at Mohali, 1995-96)

What an intriguing semi-final; a certain defeat converted into an incredible win by Mark Taylor's gallant Aussies!

Taylor decided to bat on a grassy pitch and Australia was 4 for 15; Taylor, the Waugh twins Mark and Steve and Ricky Ponting contributing four runs between them. The pace and swing of the Windies express bowlers Curtly Ambrose and Ian Bishop destroyed Australia's top order.

Rescued by a fifth wicket stand of 138 runs off 32 overs between Stuart Law (72 run out) and Michael Bevan (69), Australia totalled 8 for 207.

The Windies started brilliantly. Shivnarine Chanderpaul (80) had a 68 run partnership with Brian Lara (45) and a 72 run partnership with skipper Richie Richardson (49 not out). Chanderpaul was heading for a century but was hampered by cramps. After 41 overs they were 2 for 165, needing 43 from nine overs with eight wickets intact.

After Chanderpaul was dismissed, seven wickets were lost for 37 runs. In a mesmerising spell, Man of the Match Shane Warne took 3 for 6. Richardson was on strike when Damien Fleming bowled the final pulsating over. Richardson hit the first ball for a four and now the West Indies needed only six runs in five balls with two wickets remaining.

Richardson went for a suicidal single and Curtly Ambrose was adjudged run out by the video umpire. Last man Courtney Walsh heaved at his first ball and was bowled. Incredibly, Australia won by five runs with three balls remaining. The Windies had snatched defeat from the jaws of victory.

"It was a game we couldn't possibly win, yet we did, and is definitely the best victory I've been involved in one-day cricket," said an elated Mark Waugh.

With this win Australia entered the Final which they lost to Sri Lanka by seven wickets at Lahore.

## Extras dominate as Zimbabwe shocks India
## (India vs Zimbabwe at Leicester, 1999)

The match was a thriller with a surprise ending. It was rich in sundries, as many as 90 extras were given away; 51 by India and 39 by Zimbabwe. Sent in to bat, Zimbabwe scored 9 for 252, the Flower brothers Grant (45) and Andy (68 not out) and wides (21) dominating.

The Zimbabwe bowlers were very inaccurate, especially Henry Olonga who bowled 6 wides and Heath Streak 8 wides, as India approached their win target.

India surely missed her star batsman Sachin Tendulkar. He had flown back to India hearing of his father's sudden death. So Sadagoppan Ramesh had to open India's innings and top scored with 55, adding 99 runs in 19 overs with Ajay Jadeja (43) for the fourth wicket.

The match swung India's way when Nayan Mongia hit a quickfire 28 and tail-ender Javagal Srinath lifted two tall sixes. India needed only nine runs in two overs with three wickets in hand. But the erratic Olonga turned into a match winner dismissing India's last three batsmen off his second, fifth and final ball.

Zimbabwe won by three runs off the last ball. Grant Flower was adjudged Man of the Match. The Indian supporters' behavior was appalling as they invaded the field after the match, jostling the players and stoning the team bus.

## Shoaib's terrifying pace tilted the match Pakistan's way
## (Australia vs Pakistan at Leeds, 1999)

Inzamam-ul-Haq's 81, Shoaib Akhtar's pace-like-fire and skipper Wasim Akhtar's 4 for 40 were behind Pakistan's narrow win with only one ball remaining. Apart from his stroke play, the bulky 'Inzy' provided "entertainment" with his chaotic running between wickets. Three times he found himself at the same end as his partner and twice it cost his country a wicket – his included.

It was a widely fluctuating match with an exciting climax.

Sent in to bat Pakistan made 8 for 275 as Abdul Razzaq (60) and 'Inzy' added 118 runs for the fourth wicket.

Australia started their chase disastrously when the aggressive Adam Gilchrist was bowled by Wasim Akram for a duck. Then Mark Waugh (41) and Ricky Ponting (47) added 91 runs for the second wicket and skipper Steve Waugh (49) and Michael Bevan (61) added 113 for the fifth, defying Shoaib's electrifying speed. Both had smacked Saqlain Mushtaq (3 for 51) for sixes. The hunt was on.

In the final pulsating over Wasim Akram clean bowled Damien Martyn and Glenn McGrath and Pakistan had won the thriller by 10 runs. For his match-winning spell of 9.5-1-40-4, Akram deserved the Man of the Match award but it went to top scorer Inzamam-ul-Haq.

Skipper Steve Waugh denied the rumour that there was a rift between him and vice- captain Shane Warne. Another rumour floated that Pakistan had tampered with the ball.

## World Cup's first ever Tie
### (Australia vs South Africa at Birmingham, 1999)

This thriller was considered the best one-day international of all time. Australia was 4 for 68 in this fluctuating semi-final but was rescued by captain Steve Waugh (56) and Michael Bevan (65) who added 90 runs. Proteas fast bowlers Shaun Pollock (5 for 36) and Alan Donald (4 for 32) were magnificently incisive and Australia totalled 213.

South Africa's reply was a virtual carbon copy of Australia's. They were 4 for 61 when Jacques Kallis (53) and Jonty Rhodes (43) added 84. Man of the Match Shane Warne swung the match Australia's way with tantalizing figures of 10-4-29-4.

Then came Lance Klusener, the Man of the World Cup, on the scene and gave the match another twist. He hammered 31 unbeaten runs off 16 balls and took South Africa to the brink of their first Final. But his brain short-circuited in the last tense over.

He hit two fours off Damien Fleming to level the score. Now only one run was needed off four balls to win with Klusener on strike and experienced no. 11 bat Donald at the other end.

Knowing that a tie would be sufficient to enter the final because of Australia's better net run-rate, Steve Waugh reshuffled the field. Klusener drove the ball straight and Donald nearly got run out.

In desperation, Klusener drove the next ball and charged. A dazed Donald dropped the bat in panic and set off as an afterthought. Alas, too late. Mark Waugh at gully flicked the ball to Fleming who rolled it to Adam Gilchrist who broke the stumps, and South African hearts.

"It was the best cricket game I've ever played", a delighted Steve Waugh said. This tantalizing tie took Australia to the Final where they thrashed Pakistan at Lord's to lift the World Cup for the second time.

## Lara lights up Newlands as the Windies win the Cup opener
## (South Africa vs West Indies at Cape Town, 2002-03)

A day after a spectacular opening ceremony the host nation South Africa took on the West Indies at Newlands, Cape Town. The Windies tumbled at first to lose 2 for 7, their openers falling to skipper Shaun Pollock but then galloped as Brian Lara played a scintillating innings of 116 off 134 balls. Lara was almost out first ball but was dropped by Jacques Kallis, a difficult catch in the slip.

The lower order batsmen Ricardo Powell and Ramnaresh Sarwan attacked and 110 runs came off the last 10 overs, Pollock's penultimate over yielding 23 runs. West Indies made a challenging 5 for 278.

Gary Kirsten started off with 69. Then Mark Boucher (49) and Lance Klusener (57) attacked with gusto. Klusener reached his 50 with his fifth six. The South Africans looked set for a victory but fell three runs short.

In a match with a nail-biting finish, Lara was the deserving Man of the Match.

## Rain, a tie and D/L method eliminate South Africa
## (South Africa vs Sri Lanka at Durban, 2002-03)

It was only the second tie in World Cup cricket.

Winning the toss Sri Lanka totalled 9 for 268. Opener and subsequent Man of the Match Marvan Atapattu scored 124 and added 152 runs off 132 balls for the fourth wicket with Aravinda de Silva (73).

It started raining late in the South African innings and by the Duckworth/Lewis rule their target became 229 runs to tie in 45 overs. Sadly they had misread the fine print and thought they needed 229 to win. Opening batsman Herschelle Gibbs scored 73 and was out at 4 for 149. Mark Boucher (an aggressive and unbeaten 45) and Shaun Pollock (25) picked up the tempo but Pollock was given run out after several television replays.

Boucher hit the penultimate ball in the last and 45th over for a six thinking that South Africa had won. So he played the last soggy ball of the match defensively and did not run. Had he taken a single, South Africa would have won.

Instead, the match ended in a tie. THanks to the point system, Sri Lanka progressed to the semi-final and South Africa was eliminated.

Oh for the ifs and buts of cricket!

## A Miracle Named Bichel
## (Australia vs England at Port Elizabeth, 2002-03)

A miracle win was brought about by Australia's unsung hero Andy Bichel with help from Michael Bevan. Fast medium Bichel captured 7 for 20 in 10 accurate and penetrating overs and England was dismissed for 8 for 204 with valuable forties from Alec Stewart and Andrew Flintoff.

But with England's fast bowler Andy Caddick dismissing Australia's top four batsmen, it seemed all over for Australia. They were 8 down for 135 and the Barmy Army was on song. Then a miracle happened when tail-ender Bichel joined Bevan, perhaps the most versatile limited-overs cricketer ever. Bichel was already a hero after capturing seven scalps on a slow pitch. Now he shone out as a batsman as well.

The two Bs (Bevan 74, Bichel 34) added 73 precious runs without getting separated. Needing 14 to win in two overs, Bichel swung for a six and then a four and Australia won by two wickets with two balls to spare. Miracle maker Bichel was the undisputed Man of the Match.

Australia had won her 12th consecutive one-day international – a record then. They went on to win the World Cup defeating India in the Final by 125 runs in Johannesburg, Ponting scoring a magnificent 140 off 121 deliveries.

## Ireland shocks former champion Pakistan on a green pitch
## (Ireland vs Pakistan at Kingston, 2006-07)

The pluck of the Irish continued two days later on what was to become their favourite venue, Kingston. What a shock, what an initiation; a country playing her second World Cup match defeating the experienced and former champion Pakistan.

On a green pitch on St Patrick's Day, Ireland's captain Trent Johnston won the toss again and sent their opponents in to bat again. Pakistan floundered and was bowled out for 132, no one reaching 30. Medium-pacer Andre Botha had bowled with pinpoint accuracy, his figures were 8-4-5-2.

With Man of the Match Niall O'Brien hitting a polished 72, Ireland reached 7 for 133 in 41.4 overs to win by three wickets. And Irish eyes were smiling again

A delighted skipper Johnston had contributed hugely to start off and end off this match by winning a vital toss and hitting the winning six off Azhar Mahmood as Irish spectators exploded in delight at the surprise win.

There was tragic news hours later; the sudden death of Pakistan coach Bob Woolmer.

## Sri Lanka lose by a wicket despite Malinga's mesmerizing spell
## (South Africa vs Sri Lanka, at Guyana, 2006-07)

With Tillakaratne Dilshan (58) and Russel Arnold (50) adding 97 for the sixth wicket Sri Lanka was cruising at 5 for 195. Just then swing bowler Charl Langeveldt took control and Sri Lankans lost their last five wickets for 14 runs to be dismissed for 209 in 49.3 overs.

Aggressive skipper Graeme Smith (59) and steady-as-you-go Jacques Kallis (86) put on 94 for the second wicket. Legendary spinner Muttiah Muralitharan took three early wickets before hairy scary fast bowler with a pronounced round arm slingy action, Lasith Malinga, took over. He created history by becoming the first bowler to capture four wickets in four balls.

Malinga clean bowled Shaun Pollock for 13 off his fifth ball and had Andrew Hall caught by Tharanga in the covers for a first ball duck. End of the over. From the other end Chaminda Vaas bowled an economical over conceding only one run. Malinga dismissed the well set Kallis caught behind by Kumar Sangakkara to get his hat-trick and bowled new batsman Makhaya Ntini for a duck to achieve his unique super hat-trick (four wickets off four deliveries).

The Proteas now 9 for 207 still needed three to win.

Their bowling hero Langeveldt took a single. With two runs required for a victory Robin Peterson edged a four off the second Malinga delivery. And South Africa had won by one wicket with four balls in hand.

Malinga and Langeveldt were the joint Men of the Match.

The best compliment Malinga received was from opposing captain Graeme Smith: "He made me age a few years."

## Lara's farewell tinged with a one wicket defeat
## (England vs West Indies at Bridgetown, 2006-07)

England's Kevin Pietersen hit a dashing century and victorious skipper Michael Vaughan shone with ball and bat but it was West Indies legend Brian Lara who received maximum applause in his farewell international appearance.

Vaughan must have regretted sending West Indies to bat as their openers Chris Gayle (a blistering 79) and Devon Smith (61) put on 131 runs. Gayle's 50 came off 29 deliveries. Receiving a standing ovation, Lara hit three magnificent fours before being run out by Pietersen for 18. Marlon Samuels scored 57 and West Indies totalled 300 off 49.5 overs, Vaughan taking 3 for 39 with his loopy spin.

Vaughan opened the England batting scoring 79 and Man of the Match Pietersen a quick 100. When he was dismissed, England needed 32 runs to win from 22 balls with three wickets remaining. Off the fifth ball of the final over from Dwayne Bravo, Stuart Broad hit a two and England won by one wicket.

At the presentation Lara asked the crowd, "Have I entertained?"and he received a thunderous and unanimous YES from 22,000 present.

## Highest scoring World Cup tie
## (England vs India at Bengaluru, 2010-11)

This was the fourth and so far the last tie in the history of the World Cup.

As if saying, "What Tendulkar can do, I can do it better", England's captain Andrew Straus scored 158 runs, England's highest World Cup innings, as England chased India's 338.

The 2010-11 World Cup belonged as much to India as to their hero Sachin Tendulkar who packed stadia with his fluent stroke play and modest demeanor. He scored 120, as India compiled 338 off 49.5 overs.

In the 46th over India was going great guns at 3 for 305 with Tendulkar ably supported earlier by Gautam Gambhir hitting 51 and Yuvraj Singh (58). Tim Bresnan was the most effective bowler taking 5 for 48 and restricted the run flow by the Indians.

England boldly took up the challenge of scoring 339 – a record chase in World Cup history. Strauss (158) and Ian Bell 69 added 170 aggressive runs for the third wicket and England was in the game at 2 for 280 in the 42nd over. They needed 59 runs in eight overs, a gettable run-rate of 7.37.

But India's fast-medium bowlers Zaheer Khan and Munaf Patel took vital wickets and England needed an unlikely 29 off two overs. Fifteen runs were smashed in the 49th over as Graeme Swann and Bresnan hit sixes off Piyush Chawla. Chawla had his revenge bowling Bresnan off his last ball.

Now to the climax; 14 needed in the final over, bowled by Patel. Ajmal Shahzad hit the third ball (his first in World Cup) for a six then ran a bye. Swann took two off the fifth ball. It came down to two runs needed for an English win but could manage only one and the match was tied.

England was involved in three more heart-stoppers within 13 days, losing two of them.

## O'Brien is the hero as Ireland shocks England
### (England vs Ireland at Bengaluru, 2010-11)

England started off brilliantly being 2 for 278 on a plumb pitch as Jonathan Trott (92) and Ian Bell (81) added 167 runs in 156 balls for the third wicket. Earlier opener Kevin Pietersen had given a good start with 59 quick runs. But the rest could not maintain the tempo and England ended with 8 for 327. Fast-medium John Mooney took 4 for 63.

England's fast bowler Jimmy Anderson bowled Ireland's skipper William Porterfield off the first ball and they were in trouble at 4 for 106 (soon to become 5 for 111) when in came Kevin O'Brien to bat with a striking pink hairdo to support the Irish Cancer Society.

He attacked from the word go, reaching his 50 in 30 balls and his 100 in 50 balls. He was run out for 113 off 63 balls, smashing 13 fours and six sixes. Alex Cusack, a Brisbane born carpenter, gave O'Brien support scoring 47 and adding 162 runs for the sixth wicket off 103 balls. Both were run out. England appeared to gain an upper hand but Mooney who had earlier restricted England with his four wicket haul scored an unbeaten 33.

Helped by some poor catching by England, Ireland reached 7 for 329 in 49.1 overs and won by three wickets with five balls to spare. Kevin O'Brien was adjudged the Man of the Match – lurid pink hairstyle, six sixes and all!

## Home crowd celebrate till 2 am after Bangladesh's finest hour
## (Bangladesh vs England at Chittagong, 2010-11)

England missed their star batsman Kevin Pietersen who flew home for a hernia operation and accurate fast bowler Stuart Broad had a side strain.

Jonathan Trott scored 67 and added 109 for the fourth wicket with Eoin Morgan (63). But the steady Bangladesh attack restricted England to 225 in 49.4 overs.

Bangladesh started well being 3 for 155, opener Imrul Kayes (60) and skipper Shakib Al Hasan (32) added 82 for the fourth wicket. But once Kayes was run out, Bangladesh lost 5 for 14 runs and became 8 for 169, Ajmal Shahzad taking 3 for 43 and Graeme Swann 2 for 42 and needed 57 runs for a shock win.

Not to be perturbed, number seven batsman Mohammad Mahmudullah and no.10 bat Shafiul Islam took Bangladesh to a two wicket victory with an over to spare. It was their first home win against England.

Imrul Kayes was cheered lustily when presented the Man of the Match award. The home crowd was ecstatic and celebrated the win till 2 am.

## Boult's initial outburst derails Scotland
## (New Zealand vs Scotland at Dunedin, 2014-15)

Kiwi's left-arm quickie Trent Boult started sensationally taking two wickets off the first two balls of his first over and was near a rare hat-trick. His bowling partner Tim Southee was equally unplayable and Scotland was 4 for 12.

But they were lifted by Matt Machen (56 off 79 balls, seven fours and a six) and Richie Berrington (50 off 80 balls with four fours and a six) who added 97 runs. They were bowled out for 142 off 36.2 overs, Boult and Southee taking two wickets each and later medium pacer Corey Anderson and left-arm spinner Daniel Vettori captured three wickets each.

Kane Williamson scored 38 and Grant Elliott 29 and New Zealand totalled 7 for 146 to win by three wickets. For his initial strikes Boult was adjudged Man of the Match.

## Gladiators Gary and Kevin neutralize Shaiman's century
## (Ireland vs UAE at Brisbane, 2014-15)

Shaiman Anwar scored a brilliant 106 off 83 balls with 10 fours and a six and United Arab Emirates (UAE) totalled 9 for 278. He added 107 runs in 71 balls for the seventh wicket with Amjad Javed (42 off 35 balls hitting five fours). Earlier, opener Amjad Ali had made 45 with five fours.

Ireland started shakily being 4 for 97 but their wicket-keeper batsman Gary Wilson came to their rescue with an aggressive 80 off 69 balls, hitting nine fours. He was joined by big hitting Kevin O'Brien with 108 runs needed off 68 balls. They added 72 quick runs for the seventh wicket, Kevin smacking eight fours and two sixes in his aggressive 50 off 25 deliveries.

In panic mode, UAE misfielded and dropped catches. Ireland won by two wickets with four balls remaining. Gary Wilson was adjudged Man of the Match.

## Shenwari's sixes lead to Afghanistan's one wicket win
## (Afghanistan vs Scotland at Dunedin, 2014-15)

The match between two minor cricketing nations turned out to be an epic encounter.

Scotland started poorly losing 8 for 144. Then Majid Haq and Alasdair Evans added 62 for the ninth wicket as Scotland was all out for 210. Tall Afghani fast medium bowler Shapoor Zadran with a long run-up and longer hair took 4 for 38 and was supported by medium pacer Dawlat Zadran (3 for 29).

Opener Javed Ahmadi started off with a run-a-ball 51 enriched with eight fours but Afghanistan was soon 7 for 97. But they recovered to reach 9 for 211 and they won with a wicket and three balls to spare. The player behind the recovery and victory was Man of the Match Samiullah Shenwari.

Six-o-maniac Shenwari hit seven fours and five sixes in his 96, three of the sixes were belted in one over. This is how his sixes flew. He hit a six and a four off successive balls in the 39th over. And just when his country needed runs in a hurry, he smashed three sixes in the 47th over, the third six landing near the Afghan supporters. The crowd's hero was Shapoor Zadran who took the winning single in the last over, dropped his bat and helmet and ran 30 metres before dropping to his knees in ecstasy as the Afghan supporters chanted, "Mighty, mighty Afghans."

## Trent Boult a bolt from the blue as Kiwis win by one wicket
## (Australia vs New Zealand at Auckland, 2014-15)

Nineteen wickets fell in just 55.3 overs, the scheduled 100-over match finishing in almost half time but no one was complaining, especially the home crowd of delighted New Zealanders. A win against Australia always makes the Kiwis ecstatic.

Australia was literally swung out, crashing from 1 for 80 in 13th over to 9 for 106 in the 22nd and all out for 151 in 32.2 overs as Brad Haddin (top scorer with 43) and Pat Cummins added vital 45 for the last wicket.

The destroyers of the Aussie castle were seamers Trent Boult who had marvellous figures of 10-3-27-5 and Tim Southee (9-0-65-2).

New Zealand's captain and opening batsman Brendon McCullum played an aggressive innings of 50 at a run rate of over 200, smashing the two Mitchells – Johnson and Starc. In all, he hit seven fours and two sixes. But his dismissal signalled a collapse.

Ross Taylor and Grant Elliott fell off successive deliveries from Starc on either side of the break. New Zealand lost three wickets for one run and was 4 for 79 in the ninth over. Cool and classy batsman Kane Williamson propped up the Kiwi slide.

Corey Anderson attacked lustily, adding 52 runs with Williamson and took New Zealand to 131, now only 21 runs needed for an upset win. Then the match took a further twist as three wickets tumbled in successive overs and they were 7 for 145, needing seven runs to win with plenty of overs remaining.

Williamson was batting faultlessly but he erred in taking a single in the 23rd over from Starc, exposing the tail-enders. Adam Milne and Southee were bowled. Wisely, Boult left the last two balls from Starc alone.

It came down to this; six runs to win with only number 11 batsman Boult remaining. And what does Williamson do? He hits the first ball from Cummins for a six.

The home crowd exploded, cheering their heroes and booing the Aussies. New Zealand won by one wicket with 161 balls remaining. Despite Williamson's heroics, Boult was adjudged Man of the Match for dismantling the Australian batting.

## Guptill's ton behind Kiwis' sixth successive win
## (Bangladesh vs New Zealand at Hamilton, 2014-15)

Bangladesh's Mohammad Mahmudullah was at his prolific best smashing an unbeaten 128 runs off 123 deliveries enriched with 12 fours and three sixes. He added 90 runs for the third wicket with Soumya Sarkar (51) and 78 with Sabbir Rahman (40 off 23 balls with five fours and two sixes) for the sixth wicket.

Bangladesh totalled a competitive 7 for 288. Their skipper and slow left arm orthodox bowler Shakib Al Hasan opened the attack – a new trend down under – and took 4 for 55.

New Zealand opener Martin Guptill batted confidently and struck 105 runs (his sixth one-day international ton) off 100 balls with 11 fours and two sixes. He added 131 runs for the third wicket with Ross Taylor (56 runs off 97 balls). Later Corey Anderson hit three fours and three sixes in his 26 ball blitz of 39 runs. As a climax, tail-ender Tim Southee smashed a six and a four in the 49th over as his team reached the winning target with three wickets and seven balls remaining.

Guptill was made man of the Match. It was New Zealand's sixth win in six matches.

## Elliott's six takes New Zealand to her first Final
## (South Africa vs New Zealand at Auckland, 2014-15)

The semi-final between New Zealand and South Africa at Auckland was a thriller. In a rain-interrupted match, South Africa made 5 for 281 in 43 overs, Faf du Plessis 82 and AB de Villiers 65 not out batted well. Then with rain coming and the match reduced to 43 overs, David Miller smashed 49 off only 18 balls. Corey Anderson took 3 for 72 but proved expensive as he was hit for 12 runs per over.

New Zealand chasing a revised target of 298 runs in 43 overs was given a blistering start by McCullum scoring 59. With 94 runs needed off 70 deliveries, de Villiers squandered a run-out chance. Then with only 14 needed off seven balls Elliott was about to be caught by substitute fielder Farhaan Berhardien. As Duminy was watching the ball in the sky he did not notice Berhardien about to take the catch. The two collided and Grant Elliott got a life. Call it a comedy of errors but the Proteas did not see it that way!

Now New Zealand needed 12 runs in the final over for a thrilling climax. Elliott drove the penultimate ball from express fast bowler Dale Steyn over long-on for a six and New Zealand won by four wickets to enter the World Cup Final for the first time.

The irony of the situation was that Man of the Match Elliott was born in Johannesburg and had scored a double century for South Africa in an Under-19 match. He migrated to New Zealand in 2011.

After this surprise win, a confident New Zealand met Australia in the Final on the Melbourne Cricket Ground five days later. Australia extracted revenge for their one wicket loss at Auckland a month earlier by winning the Final by seven wickets, watched and applauded by over 90,000 mostly Aussie spectators chanting "Ozy, Ozy, Ozy; oi, oi, o."

# CRICKET WORLD CUP

## The Firsts, Mosts, Onlys and Quirkiest of the World Cup

KERSI MEHER-HOMJI AND RAJESH KUMAR

**2** The West Indies won the first two World Cups in 1975 and in 1979 and were the runners-up in 1983.

India won twice, in 1983 and 2010-11 and was runners-up in 2002-03. **2**

England were runners-up three times, in 1979, 1987-88 and 1991-92 but without winning once.

Despite being one of the strongest teams, South Africa has failed to enter the Final even once.

**1** Sri Lanka won in 1995-96 and were runners-up in 2006-07 and 2010-11.

Pakistan won in 1991-92 and were runners-up in 1999.

# The Firsts

**17** The West Indies lifted the first World Cup, beating Australia by 17 runs in the Final at Lord's on June 21, 1975.

The first World Cup, called the Prudential World Cup, was inaugurated in England on June 7, 1975 when four matches were played on the same day. **1975**

The family touch was evident in the inaugural World Cup in England. Three pairs and a trio of brothers, six sons, a pair of cousins and three nephews of well-known Test cricketers were seen in action from June 7 to 21, 1975. Australia was led by Ian Chappell and included his brother, the graceful Greg. Pakistan was represented by brothers Mushtaq and Sadiq Mohammad. New Zealand had a pair of brothers in Hedley and Geoff Howarth and a trio in Barry, Dale and Richard Hadlee, sons of former captain Walter Hadlee. All three Hadlee brothers played against England on June 11. India included Mohinder Amarnath and Anshuman Gaekwad whose fathers Lala Amarnath and Dattaji Gaekwad had captained India in Tests. Pakistan included Majid Khan and cousin Imran Khan. Majid's father Jahangir Khan had represented India in four Tests including the inaugural Lord's Test in 1932. Asif Iqbal is the nephew of India's Test off-spinner Ghulam Ahmed. India's Sunil Gavaskar is the nephew of Test wicket-keeper Madhav Mantri. The West Indies team included skipper Clive Lloyd and his cousin Lance Gibbs.

The first total of over 350 came in the 1987-88 World Cup, when West Indies amassed 4 for 360 in 50 overs against Sri Lanka at Karachi on October 13, the master blaster Viv Richards hammering 181.

**400** The first total of over 400 was recorded by India (5 for 413) against Bermuda at Port-of-Spain on March 19, 2007.

England's Dennis Amiss (137 against India at Lord's) was the first to post a century on June 7, 1975. A few minutes later New Zealander Glenn Turner scored 171 not out against East Africa at Birmingham. **100**

**1000** Viv Richards was the first to aggregate 1000 runs (1013 at 63.31 in 23 matches) and the first to hit three centuries. His 1000th run came against Pakistan during his 21st innings at Karachi on October 30, 1987.

**2000**

Tendulkar was the first and only batsman to aggregate 2000 runs in the World Cup, 2278 at 56.95 in 45 matches.

**1000**

Sachin Tendulkar was the quickest to 1000 runs, accomplishing the feat in his 20th innings - his aggregate at the end of the innings against Pakistan at Manchester on June 8, 1999 being 1043 at 61.35.  South Africa's Abraham de Villiers had emulated Tendulkar's feat of reaching the milestone in 20 innings - his tally at the end of the innings against Pakistan at Auckland on March 7, 2015 being the same, 1043 at 57.94.

Holland's Feiko Kloppenburg was the first all-rounder to achieve the double of a century (121 runs) and 4 wickets (4 for 42) in the same match. This was against Namibia at Bloemfontein on March 3, 2003 where he had opened the batting and bowled medium pace. [Sri Lanka's Tillakaratne Dilshan, with 144 runs and four for four against Zimbabwe at Kandy on March 10, 2011, became the second all-rounder to accomplish the double of a century and bag four wickets in the same World Cup match.]

**5**

Australia's Dennis Lillee was the first to grab five wickets in an innings, 5 for 34 against Pakistan at Leeds, on June 7, 1975.

Australia's Mark Waugh (130) and his twin brother Steve (82) were the first to be associated in a double century partnership; 207 runs for the third wicket against Kenya at Visakhapatnam on February 23, 1996.

**200**

West Indies's aggressive opener Chris Gayle was the first to score a double century, 215 against Zimbabwe at Canberra on February 24, 2015.

India's Sourav Ganguly (183) and Rahul Dravid (145) were the first to add 300 runs, (318) for the second wicket against Sri Lanka at Taunton, England on May 26, 1999.

**300**

**7**

West Indian Winston Davis became the first bowler to claim seven wickets in an innings, 7 for 51 against Australia at Leeds on June 11 and 12, 1983.

# Mosts

England has hosted the most number of World Cups, four – the first three in 1975, 1979, 1983 – and in 1999. It will host the fifth one in 2019.

AB de Villiers (South Africa) and Chris Gayle (West Indies) have hit most sixes, 37 each; de Villiers in 23 matches, Gayle in 26.

Tendulkar was adjudged the Man of the Match most frequently, nine times in 45 matches. The next best is Glenn McGrath, six times in 39 matches. Lance Klusener of South Africa leads on percentage, being made Man of the Match five times in 14 matches, a percentage of 35.71.

**84** Australia has played most World Cup matches, 84 and won most, 62 and achieving the best win percentage of 75.30. The next best win percentage is 65.45 by South Africa.

**275** Australia has won by the biggest runs' margin, 275 runs against Afghanistan at Perth on March 4, 2015. This remains their biggest win by runs' margin in ODIs.

Australia's Ricky Ponting has played most matches, 46.

India's Sachin Tendulkar scored most runs in one World Cup, 673 at an average of 61.18 in 11 matches in 2002-03. **673**

New Zealand's Martin Guptill recorded the highest score, 237 not out against the West Indies at Wellington on March 21, 2015. The only other double centurion is Chris Gayle of West Indies, 215 against Zimbabwe at Canberra on February 24, 2015.

**124** South Africa's Lance Klusener has the highest batting average (124.00) and best strike-rate (121.17) while scoring 372 runs in eleven innings (eight times not out). He remains the only batsman to have averaged 100-plus apart from maintaining Strike Rate of 100-plus in the history of the World Cup.

Gayle's 138-ball knock (215) against Zimbabwe at Canberra on February 24, 2015 remains the quickest double century in the history of ODIs. He had outstripped Virender Sehwag's 140-ball 219 against West Indies at Indore on December 8, 2011.

**215**

Sixteen sixes hit by Chris Gayle in the above innings are the joint-most by a batsman in the history of ODIs. Rohit Sharma had recorded the same number of sixes during his innings of 209 off 158 balls against Australia at Bengaluru on November 2, 2013 and AB de Villiers hit 16 during his magnificent 149 off 44 balls against West Indies at Johannesburg on January 18, 2015.

Most runs scored without the fall of a wicket: 344. In the match between Pakistan and the West Indies in Melbourne on February 23, 1992, Pakistan scored 2 for 220 and the West Indies replied with none for 221 to win by 10 wickets. Amazingly, the last 344 runs were amassed without the loss of a wicket!

Gayle and Marlon Samuels were engaged in the highest partnership, 372 runs for the second wicket, West Indies against Zimbabwe at Canberra on February 24, 2015. This stand remains the highest partnership for any wicket in ODIs.

With Marlon Samuels also scoring an unbeaten 133 in the above match, that occasion provided the first instance in the history of World Cup/ODIs when a double century and a century have been recorded in the same innings. (On July 20, 2018, the Pakistani openers, Fakhar Zaman (210 not out) and Imam-ul-Haq (113) provided the second instance - against Zimbabwe at Bulawayo).

The 298 balls faced by Gayle and Samuels to set a world-record partnership (for any wicket) of 372 for the second wicket are the most faced by a pair in the history of ODIs, outstripping the 278 balls faced by Sachin Tendulkar and Rahul Dravid during their second-wicket partnership of 331 vs New Zealand at Hyderabad on November 8, 1999.

Australia's Glenn McGrath has the best bowling spell, 7 for 15 vs Namibia at Potchefstroom on February 27, 2003.

Sri Lanka's Lasith Malinga has the best Strike Rate, 23.8 while taking 43 wickets in 22 matches (minimum qualification: 40 wickets). He has also taken most hat-tricks, two.

West Indian Andy Roberts has the best Economy Rate, 3.24 in 16 matches while taking 26 wickets (minimum qualification: 25 wickets).

Australia's Adam Gilchrist has taken most catches, 45 (out of 52 dismissals, stumpings seven) in 31 matches.

Sri Lanka's Kumar Sangakkara effected most dismissals, 54 (41 catches and 13 stumpings) in 37 matches.

# Onlys

Sachin Tendulkar is the only player to hit six centuries and 15 fifties.

**673** He is also the only one to record over 500 runs in two editions of the World Cup; 673 at an average of 61.18 in 11 matches in 2002-03 and 523 at 87.16 in seven matches in 1995-96.

He is also the only one to hit over 200 fours, 241. Next best are Kumar Sangakkara, 147 fours and Ricky Ponting 145. **241**

Sri Lanka's Lasith Malinga is the only one to perform two hat-tricks; on March 28, 2007 against South Africa at Georgetown, Providence Stadium, Guyana (West Indies) and on March 1, 2011 against Kenya at Colombo RPS (Sri Lanka).

**4in4** Malinga's first hat-trick (in 2006-07) was a 'super' hat-trick, four wickets in four balls – his victims being Shaun Pollock, Andrew Hall, Jacques Kallis and Makhaya Ntini.

Chaminda Vaas' spell for Sri Lanka against Bangladesh at Pietermaritzburg on Valentine's Day 2003 is unique in any form of cricket. He started the match by taking a hat-trick. To quote Wisden 2004, "Vaas's celebration was appropriately wild: he looked like an aeroplane piloted by a drunkard." By dismissing Hannan Sarkar, Mohammad Ashraful and Ehsanul Haque, Vaas became the first ever bowler to bag three wickets off the first three deliveries in an ODI.

**6x6** South Africa's Herschelle Gibbs is the only one to hit 6 sixes in an over, (6, 6, 6, 6, 6, 6), in any international match. This was off Daan van Bunge from Holland at Basseterre on March 16, 2007.

By hitting 105 not out against Bangladesh at Melbourne on February 26; 117 not out vs England at Wellington on March 1; 104 vs Australia at Sydney on March 8 and 124 vs Scotland at Hobart on March 11 in the 2015 World Cup, Sangakkara remains the only batsman to register four successive centuries in the history of the World Cup. **4**

# Quirkiest

Minnows Kenya shocked the then mighty West Indies (which included Brian Lara, Richie Richardson, Curtly Ambrose and Courtney Walsh) by 73 runs in Pune, India, in the 1995-96 World Cup. With Maurice Odumbe claiming 3 for 15 and Rajab Ali 3 for 17, the Windies were dismissed for 93.

**93**

**111**

In the 2002-03 World Cup Canada's John Davison stunned the West Indies with a fast century, smashing six sixes and eight fours in a brilliant 111 from 76 balls at Centurion, the only hundred by a Canadian batsman in the World Cup. To quote Wisden 2004, "He batted like a millionaire, clobbering a sensational hundred in just 67 balls." He followed this with a quick-fire 75 off 62 balls against New Zealand at Benoni nine days later, his 50 coming off just 25 balls. Despite his scintillating batting and bowling and being adjudged Man of the Match, Canada lost both times.

When asked who can beat Australia in the 2006-07 World Cup, the West Indies legend Viv Richards quipped, "Salmonella poisoning!"

**87**

Underdogs Bangladesh upset two strong teams in the 2006-07 World Cup, beating India by five wickets at Port-of-Spain and South Africa by 67 runs three weeks later at Providence, Guyana. Man of the Match Mohammad Ashraful was the top scorer in the match, making 87.

Australia's fast-medium bowler Andy Bichel's spell of 7 for 20 (against England at Port Elizabeth in the 2002-03 World Cup) is the second best spell of bowling after Glenn McGrath's 7 for 15. Bichel also averaged 117.00 with the bat scoring 117 runs in three innings, twice not out, highest score 64 vs New Zealand at Port Elizabeth on March 11, 2003. Cricket, quirky cricket! Bichel's 64 is the highest individual score by a player batting at number 9 or lower at the World Cup.

None of the five West Indies express fast bowlers – Malcolm Marshall, Andy Roberts, Michael Holding, Curtly Ambrose and Courtney Walsh – could manage a five-wicket per innings haul despite playing 72 World Cup matches between them. The best bowling spell for a West Indian is by fast bowler Winston Davis who took 7 for 51 against Australia at Headingley in the 1983 World Cup. Remarkably, it was his debut in the World Cup.

# World Cup records - 1975 to 2015

RAJESH KUMAR

## Team Records
## Results Summary

| Team | First game | P | W | L | NR | T | Winning % | Titles | Title wins |
|------|-----------|---|---|---|----|----|-----------|--------|------------|
| Australia | 7.6.1975 | 84 | 62 | 20 | 1 | 1 | 75.30 | 5 | 1987, 1999, 2003, 2007 & 2015 |
| South Africa | 26.2.1992 | 55 | 35 | 18 | - | 2 | 65.45 | - | |
| India | 7.6.1975 | 75 | 46 | 27 | 1 | 1 | 62.83 | 2 | 1983 & 2011 |
| New Zealand | 7.6.1975 | 79 | 48 | 30 | 1 | - | 61.53 | - | |
| West Indies | 7.6.1975 | 71 | 41 | 29 | 1 | - | 58.57 | 2 | 1975 & 1979 |
| England | 7.6.1975 | 72 | 41 | 29 | 1 | 1 | 58.45 | - | |
| Pakistan | 7.6.1975 | 71 | 40 | 29 | 2 | - | 57.97 | 1 | 1992 |
| Sri Lanka | 7.6.1975 | 73 | 35 | 35 | 2 | 1 | 50.00 | 1 | 1996 |
| Ireland | 15.3.2007 | 21 | 7 | 13 | - | 1 | 35.71 | - | |
| Bangladesh | 17.5.1999 | 32 | 11 | 20 | 1 | - | 35.48 | - | |
| Kenya | 18.2.1996 | 29 | 6 | 22 | 1 | - | 21.42 | - | |
| Zimbabwe | 9.6.1983 | 57 | 11 | 42 | 3 | 1 | 21.29 | - | |
| Afghanistan | 18.2.2015 | 6 | 1 | 5 | - | - | 16.66 | - | |
| Canada | 9.6.1979 | 18 | 2 | 16 | - | - | 11.11 | - | |
| Netherlands | 17.2.1996 | 20 | 2 | 18 | - | - | 10.00 | - | |
| U.A.E. | 16.2.1996 | 11 | 1 | 10 | - | - | 9.09 | - | |
| East Africa | 7.6.1975 | 3 | - | 3 | - | - | 0.00 | - | |
| Scotland | 16.5.1999 | 14 | - | 14 | - | - | 0.00 | - | |
| Namibia | 10.2.2003 | 6 | - | 6 | - | - | 0.00 | - | |
| Bermuda | 15.3.2007 | 3 | - | 3 | - | - | 0.00 | - | |

## World Cup Finals - Results Summary

| Date | Toss | Venue | Winning Team | Batting | Losing Team | Winning Captain | Margin |
|------|------|-------|--------------|---------|-------------|-----------------|--------|
| 21-6-1975 | Aus | Lord's | W.Indies | First | Australia | Clive Lloyd | 17 runs |
| 23-6-1979 | Eng | Lord's | W.Indies | First | England | Clive Lloyd | 92 runs |
| 25-6-1983 | WI | Lord's | India | First | W.Indies | Kapil Dev | 43 runs |
| 8-11-1987 | Aus | Kolkata | Australia | First | England | Allan Border | 7 runs |
| 25-3-1992 | Pak | Melbourne | Pakistan | First | England | Imran Khan | 22 runs |
| 17-3-1996 | SL | Lahore | S.Lanka | Second | Australia | Arjuna Ranatunga | 7 wickets |
| 20-6-1999 | Pak | Lord's | Australia | Second | Pakistan | Steve Waugh | 8 wickets |
| 23-3-2003 | Ind | Johannesburg | Australia | First | India | Ricky Ponting | 125 runs |
| 28-4-2007 | Aus | Bridgetown | Australia | First | S.Lanka | Ricky Ponting | 53 runs |
| 2-4-2011 | SL | Mumbai | India | Second | S.Lanka | Mahendra S Dhoni | 6 wickets |
| 29-3-2015 | NZ | Melbourne | Australia | Second | N.Zealand | Michael Clarke | 7 wickets |

# Highest Innings Totals (360 and above)

| Runs | Overs | RR | For | Opponents | Venue | Date | Won by |
|------|-------|------|--------------|--------------|---------------|------------|--------------|
| 417-6 | 50.0 | 8.34 | Australia | Afghanistan | Perth | 4.3.2015 | Australia |
| 413-5 | 50.0 | 8.26 | India | Bermuda | Port of Spain | 19.3.2007 | India |
| 411-4 | 50.0 | 8.22 | South Africa | Ireland | Canberra | 3.3.2015 | South Africa |
| 408-5 | 50.0 | 8.16 | South Africa | West Indies | Sydney | 27.2.2015 | South Africa |
| 398-5 | 50.0 | 7.96 | Sri Lanka | Kenya | Kandy | 6.3.1996 | Sri Lanka |
| 393-6 | 50.0 | 7.86 | New Zealand | West Indies | Wellington | 21.3.2015 | New Zealand |
| 377-6 | 50.0 | 7.54 | Australia | South Africa | Basseterre | 24.3.2007 | Australia |
| 376-9 | 50.0 | 7.52 | Australia | Sri Lanka | Sydney | 8.3.2015 | Australia |
| 373-6 | 50.0 | 7.46 | India | Sri Lanka | Taunton | 26.5.1999 | India |
| 372-2 | 50.0 | 7.44 | West Indies | Zimbabwe | Canberra | 24.2.2015 | West Indies |
| 370-4 | 50.0 | 7.40 | India | Bangladesh | Dhaka | 19.2.2011 | India |
| 363-5 | 50.0 | 7.26 | New Zealand | Canada | Gros Islet | 22.3.2007 | New Zealand |
| 363-9 | 50.0 | 7.26 | Sri Lanka | Scotland | Hobart | 11.3.2015 | Sri Lanka |
| 360-4 | 50.0 | 7.20 | West Indies | Sri Lanka | Karachi | 13.10.1987 | West Indies |

# Highest successful chases

| Runs | Overs | RR | For | Opponents | Venue | Date |
|-------|-------|------|------------|-------------|---------------|------------|
| 329-7 | 49.1 | 6.69 | Ireland | England | Bengaluru | 2.3.2011 |
| 322-4 | 48.1 | 6.68 | Bangladesh | Scotland | Nelson | 5.3.2015 |
| 313-7 | 49.2 | 6.34 | Sri Lanka | Zimbabwe | New Plymouth | 23.2.1992 |
| 312-1 | 47.2 | 6.59 | Sri Lanka | England | Wellington | 1.3.2015 |
| 307-4 | 47.4 | 6.44 | Ireland | Netherlands | Kolkata | 18.3.2011 |
| 307-6 | 45.5 | 6.69 | Ireland | West Indies | Nelson | 16.2.2015 |
| 301-9 | 49.5 | 6.04 | England | West Indies | Bridgetown | 21.4.2007 |
| 300-7 | 49.4 | 6.04 | S.Africa | India | Nagpur | 12.3.2011 |
| 299-6 | 42.5 | 6.98 | England | South Africa | Auckland | 24.3.2015 |

# Highest Match aggregates

| Aggregate | Overs | 1st Team | Score | 2nd Team | Score | Venue | Date |
|-----------|-------|-----------|-------|-----------|-------|------------|------------|
| 688-18 | 96.2 | Australia | 376/9 | Sri Lanka | 312 | Sydney | 8.3.2015 |
| 676-18 | 99.5 | India | 338 | England | 338-8 | Bangalore | 27.2.2011 |
| 671-16 | 98.0 | Australia | 377-6 | S.Africa | 294 | Basseterre | 24.3.2007 |
| 661-12 | 94.3 | W.Indies | 372-2 | Zimbabwe | 289 | Canberra | 24.2.2015 |
| 657-18 | 99.3 | England | 327-8 | Ireland | 329-7 | Hobart | 7.3.2015 |
| 656-15 | 99.1 | England | 327-8 | Ireland | 329-7 | Bangalore | 2.3.2011 |

# World Cup records - 1975 to 2015

RAJESH KUMAR

## Lowest completed Innings totals

| Score | Overs | For | Opponents | Venue | Date | Won by |
|---|---|---|---|---|---|---|
| 36 | 18.4 | Canada | Sri Lanka | Paarl | 19.2.2003 | S.Lanka |
| 45 | 40.3 | Canada | England | Manchester | 13.6.1979 | England |
| 45 | 14.0 | Namibia | Australia | Potchefstroom | 27.2.2003 | Australia |
| 58 | 18.5 | Bangladesh | W.Indies | Dhaka | 4.3.2011 | W.Indies |
| 68 | 31.3 | Scotland | W.Indies | Leicester | 27.5.1999 | W.Indies |
| 69 | 23.5 | Kenya | N.Zealand | Chennai | 20.2.2011 | N.Zealand |
| 74 | 40.2 | Pakistan | England | Adelaide | 1.3.1992 | No Result |
| 77 | 27.4 | Ireland | S.Lanka | St.George's | 18.4.2007 | S.Lanka |

## Lowest scores to include a hundred

| Score | Runs | Batsman | For | Opponent | Venue | Date |
|---|---|---|---|---|---|---|
| 167/3 | 119* | Ramiz Raja | Pakistan | New Zealand | Christchurch | 18-3-1992 |
| 178/1 | 102* | Stephen Fleming | N.Zealand | Bangladesh | North Sound | 2-4-2007 |
| 190/2 | 102* | Shivnarine Chanderpaul | W.Indies | Ireland | Kingston | 23-3-2007 |
| 194/1 | 106* | Gordon Greenidge | W.Indies | India | Birmingham | 9-6-1979 |

## Lowest match aggregates

| Aggregate | Overs | RR | 1st Team | Score | 2nd Team | Score | Venue | Date |
|---|---|---|---|---|---|---|---|---|
| 73-11 | 23.2 | 3.12 | Canada | 36 | S.Lanka | 37-1 | Paarl | 19.2.2003 |
| 91-12 | 54.2 | 1.67 | Canada | 45 | England | 46-2 | Manchester | 13.6.1979 |
| 117-11 | 31.1 | 3.75 | Bangladesh | 58 | W.Indies | 59-1 | Dhaka | 4.3.2011 |
| 138-12 | 41.4 | 3.31 | Scotland | 68 | W.Indies | 70-2 | Leicester | 27.5.1999 |
| 141-10 | 31.5 | 4.42 | Kenya | 69 | N.Zealand | 72-0 | Chennai | 20.2.2011 |

## Victories by biggest margins
By 230 runs or more

| Margin | Winner | Score | Loser | | Venue | Date |
|---|---|---|---|---|---|---|
| 275 runs | Australia | (417-6) | Afghanistan | (142) | Perth | 4.3.2015 |
| 257 runs | India | (413-5) | Bermuda | (156) | Port of Spain | 19.3.2007 |
| 257 runs | South Africa | (408-5) | W.Indies | (151) | Sydney | 27.2.2015 |
| 256 runs | Australia | (301-6) | Namibia | (45) | Potchefstroom | 27.2.2003 |
| 243 runs | Sri Lanka | (321-6) | Bermuda | (78) | Port of Spain | 15.3.2007 |
| 231 runs | S.Africa | (351-5) | Netherlands | (120) | Mohali | 3.3.2011 |

## Victories by biggest margins
### By 10 wickets

| Wkts. | Winner | Score | Loser | | Venue | Date |
|---|---|---|---|---|---|---|
| 10 wkts | India | (123-0) | E.Africa | (120) | Leeds | 11.6.1975 |
| 10 wkts | W.Indies | (172-0) | Zimbabwe | (171) | Birmingham | 20.6.1983 |
| 10 wkts | W.Indies | (221-0) | Pakistan | (220-2) | Melbourne | 23.2.1992 |
| 10 wkts | S.Africa | (142-0) | Kenya | (140) | Potchefstroom | 12.2.2003 |
| 10 wkts | S.Lanka | (126-0) | Bangladesh | (124) | Pietermaritzburg | 14.2.2003 |
| 10 wkts | S.Africa | (109-0) | Bangladesh | (108) | Bloemfontein | 22.2.2003 |
| 10 wkts | Australia | (106-0) | Bangladesh | (104-6) | North Sound | 31.3.2007 |
| 10 wkts | New Zealand | (72-0) | Kenya | (69) | Chennai | 20.2.2011 |
| 10 wkts | New Zealand | (166-0) | Zimbabwe | (162) | Ahmedabad | 4.3.2011 |
| 10 wkts | Pakistan | (113-0) | W.Indies | (112) | Dhaka | 23.3.2011 |
| 10 wkts | Sri Lanka | (231-0) | England | (229-6) | Colombo (RPS) | 26.3.2011 |

## Victories by smallest margins
### By runs' margin

| Margin | Winner | Loser | Venue | Date |
|---|---|---|---|---|
| 1 run | Australia | India | Madras | 9.10.1987 |
| 1 run | Australia | India | Brisbane | 1.3.1992 |
| 2 runs | Sri Lanka | England | North Sound | 4.4.2007 |
| 3 runs | New Zealand | Zimbabwe | Hyderabad | 10.10.1987 |
| 3 runs | Australia | New Zealand | Indore | 18.10.1987 |
| 3 runs | Zimbabwe | India | Leicester | 19.5.1999 |
| 3 runs | West Indies | South Africa | Cape Town | 9.2.2003 |

## By one wicket margin

| Margin | Winner | Loser | Venue | Date |
|---|---|---|---|---|
| 1 wicket | West Indies | Pakistan | Birmingham | 11.6.1975 |
| 1 wicket | Pakistan | West Indies | Lahore | 16.10.1987 |
| 1 wicket | South Africa | Sri Lanka | Providence | 28.3.2007 |
| 1 wicket | England | West Indies | Bridgetown | 21.4.2007 |
| 1 wicket | Afghanistan | Scotland | Dunedin | 26.2.2015 |
| 1 wicket | New Zealand | Australia | Auckland | 28.2.2015 |

## Tied matches

| First Team | Score | Overs | Second Team | Score | Overs | Venue | Date |
|---|---|---|---|---|---|---|---|
| Australia | 213 | 49.2 | S.Africa | 213 | 49.4 | Birmingham | 17-6-1999 |
| Sri Lanka | 268-9 | 50.0 | S.Africa | 229-6 | 45.0 | Durban | 3-3-2003 (D/L method) |
| Ireland | 221-9 | 50.0 | Zimbabwe | 221 | 50.0 | Kingston | 15-3-2007 |

# World Cup records - 1975 to 2015
RAJESH KUMAR

## Extras top-scoring in an innings

| Extras | Score | Team | Opponent | Venue | Date |
|---|---|---|---|---|---|
| 37 | 166 | Kenya | West Indies | Pune | 29-2-1996 |
| 28 | 163 | Zimbabwe | South Africa | Canberra | 10-3-1992 |
| 40 | 156 | Netherlands | Pakistan | Paarl | 25-2-2003 |
| 29 | 132 | Pakistan | Ireland | Kingston | 17-3-2007 |
| 25 | 132 | Pakistan | Australia | Lord's | 20-6-1999 |
| 15 | 45 | Namibia | Australia | Potchefstroom | 27-2-2003 |

## Most sixes in a team innings

| 6s | 4s | Score | For | Opponent | Venue | Date |
|---|---|---|---|---|---|---|
| 19 | 21 | 372/2 | West Indies | Zimbabwe | Canberra | 24-2-2015 |
| 18 | 30 | 351/3 | South Africa | Netherlands | Basseterre | 16-3-2007 |
| 18 | 30 | 413/5 | India | Bermuda | Port of Spain | 19-3-2007 |
| 16 | 27 | 349 | Pakistan | Zimbabwe | Kingston | 21-3-2007 |
| 16 | 23 | 250 | West Indies | New Zealand | Wellington | 21-3-2015 |
| 15 | 39 | 393/6 | New Zealand | West Indies | Wellington | 21-3-2015 |

## Most sixes in a match

| 6s | 4s | Teams and Sixes | Venue | Date |
|---|---|---|---|---|
| 31 | 62 | West Indies (16) & New Zealand (15) | Wellington | 21-3-2015 |
| 22 | 31 | Pakistan (16) & Zimbabwe (6) | Kingston | 21-3-2007 |
| 22 | 49 | West Indies (19) & Zimbabwe (3) | Canberra | 24-2-2015 |
| 21 | 63 | Sri Lanka (14) & Kenya (7) | Kandy | 6-3-1996 |
| 21 | 47 | South Africa (14) & Zimbabwe (7) | Hamilton | 15-2-2015 |
| 20 | 45 | India (18) & Bermuda (2) | Port of Spain | 19-3-2007 |

# Individual Records

## Batting - The leading run-getters

| Batsman | For | Runs | Ave. | 100 | 50 | HS | SR | M | I |
|---|---|---|---|---|---|---|---|---|---|
| Sachin Tendulkar | India | 2278 | 56.95 | 6 | 15 | 152 | 88.98 | 45 | 44 |
| Ricky Ponting | Aus. | 1743 | 45.86 | 5 | 6 | 140* | 79.95 | 46 | 42 |
| Kumar Sangakkara | SL | 1532 | 56.74 | 5 | 7 | 124 | 86.55 | 37 | 35 |
| Brian Lara | WI | 1225 | 42.24 | 2 | 7 | 116 | 86.26 | 34 | 33 |
| Abraham de Villiers | SA | 1207 | 63.52 | 4 | 6 | 162* | 117.29 | 23 | 22 |
| Sanath Jayasuriya | SL | 1165 | 34.26 | 3 | 6 | 120 | 90.66 | 38 | 37 |
| Jacques Kallis | SA | 1148 | 45.92 | 1 | 9 | 128* | 74.40 | 36 | 32 |

## Most runs in wins

| Batsman | For | Runs | Ave. | 100 | | HS | SR | M | I |
|---|---|---|---|---|---|---|---|---|---|
| Sachin Tendulkar | India | 1516 | 65.91 | 3 | 12 | 152 | 90.50 | 27 | 27 |
| Ricky Ponting | Aus | 1342 | 43.29 | 3 | 6 | 140* | 81.43 | 38 | 35 |
| Adam Gilchrist | Aus | 1051 | 38.92 | 1 | 8 | 149 | 101.35 | 28 | 28 |
| Kumar Sangakkara | SL | 992 | 66.13 | 4 | 5 | 124 | 95.11 | 23 | 21 |
| Matthew Hayden | Aus | 987 | 51.94 | 3 | 2 | 158 | 92.93 | 22 | 21 |
| Sanath Jayasuriya | SL | 939 | 44.71 | 3 | 5 | 120 | 96.90 | 23 | 23 |

## Highest strike rate
(minimum 700 runs)

| Batsman | For | S.R. | Runs | HS | Ave. | M | I |
|---|---|---|---|---|---|---|---|
| Brendon McCullum | NZ | 120.84 | 742 | 101 | 33.72 | 34 | 27 |
| Abraham de Villiers | SA | 117.29 | 1207 | 162* | 63.52 | 23 | 22 |
| Virender Sehwag | India | 106.17 | 843 | 175 | 38.31 | 22 | 22 |
| Adam Gilchrist | Aus | 98.01 | 1085 | 149 | 36.16 | 31 | 31 |
| Michael Clarke | Aus | 94.16 | 888 | 93* | 63.42 | 25 | 21 |

## Highest strike rate in an innings
(minimum 50 runs)

| Batsman | For | Runs | Balls | SR | Opponent | Venue | Date |
|---|---|---|---|---|---|---|---|
| Brendon McCullum | NZ | 77 | 25 | 308.00 | England | Wellington | 20-2-2015 |
| Brendon McCullum | NZ | 52* | 21 | 247.61 | Canada | Gros Islet | 22-3-2007 |
| Abraham de Villiers | SA | 162* | 66 | 245.45 | W.Indies | Sydney | 27-2-2015 |
| Angelo Matthews | SL | 51 | 21 | 242.85 | Scotland | Hobart | 11-3-2015 |
| Mark Boucher | SA | 75* | 31 | 241.93 | Netherlands | Basseterre | 16-3-2007 |

# World Cup records - 1975 to 2015
RAJESH KUMAR

## Most runs in a competition
**500 runs or more**

| Batsman | For | Runs | Ave. | 100 | 50 | SR | Season | M |
|---|---|---|---|---|---|---|---|---|
| Sachin Tendulkar | India | 673 | 61.18 | 1 | 6 | 89.25 | 2002-03 | 11 |
| Matthew Hayden | Aus. | 659 | 73.22 | 3 | 1 | 101.07 | 2006-07 | 11 |
| Mahela Jayawardene | SL | 548 | 60.88 | 1 | 4 | 85.09 | 2006-07 | 11 |
| Martin Guptill | NZ | 547 | 68.37 | 2 | 1 | 104.58 | 2014-15 | 9 |
| Kumar Sangakkara | SL | 541 | 108.20 | 4 | 0 | 105.87 | 2014-15 | 7 |
| Ricky Ponting | Aus. | 539 | 67.37 | 1 | 4 | 95.39 | 2006-07 | 11 |
| Sachin Tendulkar | India | 523 | 87.16 | 2 | 3 | 85.87 | 1995-96 | 7 |
| Tillakaratne Dilshan | SL | 500 | 62.50 | 2 | 2 | 90.74 | 2010-11 | 9 |

## Most Hundreds

| Batsman | For | 100 | Innings |
|---|---|---|---|
| Sachin Tendulkar | India | 6 | 44 |
| Kumar Sangakkara | SL | 5 | 35 |
| Ricky Ponting | Aus. | 5 | 42 |
| Sourav Ganguly | India | 4 | 21 |
| Mark Waugh | Aus. | 4 | 22 |
| Abraham de Villiers | SA | 4 | 22 |
| Tillakaratne Dilshan | SL | 4 | 25 |
| Mahela Jayawardene | SL | 4 | 34 |

## Four hundreds in successive innings

| Batsman | For | Runs | Balls | Opponent | Venue | Date |
|---|---|---|---|---|---|---|
| Kumar Sangakkara | SL | 105* | 76 | Bangladesh | Melbourne | 26-2-2015 |
| | | 117* | 86 | England | Wellington | 1-3-2015 |
| | | 104 | 107 | Australia | Sydney | 8-3-2015 |
| | | 124 | 95 | Scotland | Hobart | 11-3-2015 |

## Highest individual innings

| Runs | Balls | Batsman | For | Opponent | Venue | Date |
|---|---|---|---|---|---|---|
| 237* | 163 | Martin Guptill | N.Zealand | W.Indies | Wellington | 21.3.2015 |
| 215 | 147 | Chris Gayle | W.Indies | Zimbabwe | Canberra | 24.2.2015 |
| 188* | 159 | Gary Kirsten | S.Africa | UAE | Rawalpindi | 16.2.1996 |
| 183 | 158 | Sourav Ganguly | India | S.Lanka | Taunton | 26.5.1999 |
| 181 | 125 | Vivian Richards | W.Indies | S.Lanka | Karachi | 13.10.1987 |
| 178 | 133 | David Warner | Australia | Afghanistan | Perth | 4.3.2015 |
| 175* | 138 | Kapil Dev | India | Zimbabwe | Tunbridge Wells | 18.6.1983 |
| 175 | 140 | Virender Sehwag | India | Bangladesh | Dhaka | 19.2.2011 |

# Centuries on the first day of a World Cup competition

| Runs | Balls | Batsman | For | Opponent | Venue | Date |
|------|-------|---------|-----|----------|-------|------|
| 137 | 147 | Dennis Amiss | England | India | Lord's | 7-6-1975 |
| 171* | 201 | Glenn Turner | N.Zealand | East Africa | Birmingham | 7-6-1975 |
| 106* | 173 | Gordon Greenidge | W.Indies | India | Birmingham | 9-6-1979 |
| 102 | 105 | Allan Lamb | England | New Zealand | The Oval | 9-6-1983 |
| 103 | 100 | Javed Miandad | Pakistan | Sri Lanka | Hyderabad | 8-10-1987 |
| 100* | 134 | Martin Crowe | N.Zealand | Australia | Auckland | 22-2-1992 |
| 100 | 133 | David Boon | Australia | New Zealand | Auckland | 22-2-1992 |
| 101 | 132 | Nathan Astle | N.Zealand | England | Ahmedabad | 14-2-1996 |
| 116 | 134 | Brian Lara | W.Indies | South Africa | Cape Town | 9-2-2003 |
| 175 | 140 | Virender Sehwag | India | Bangladesh | Dhaka | 19-2-2011 |
| 100* | 83 | Virat Kohli | India | Bangladesh | Dhaka | 19-2-2011 |
| 135 | 128 | Aaron Finch | Australia | England | Melbourne | 14-2-2015 |

# Nervous 99

| Runs | Balls | SR | Batsman | For | Opponent | Venue | Date |
|------|-------|-----|---------|-----|----------|-------|------|
| 99 | 88 | 112.50 | Adam Gilchrist | Australia | S.Lanka | Centurion | 7.3.2003 |
| 99 | 103 | 96.11 | Jean-Paul Duminy | S.Africa | Ireland | Kolkata | 15.3.2011 |
| 99 | 82 | 120.73 | Abraham de Villiers | S.Africa | UAE | Wellington | 12.3.2015 |

# Highest score at each batting position

| No. | Runs | Balls | Batsman | For | Opponent | Venue | Date |
|-----|------|-------|---------|-----|----------|-------|------|
| 1 | 237* | 163 | Martin Guptill | N.Zealand | W.Indies | Wellington | 21.3.2015 |
| 2 | 215 | 147 | Chris Gayle | W.Indies | Zimbabwe | Canberra | 24.2.2015 |
| 3 | 145 | 129 | Rahul Dravid | India | S.Lanka | Taunton | 26.5.1999 |
| 4 | 181 | 125 | Vivian Richards | W.Indies | S.Lanka | Karachi | 13.10.1987 |
| 5 | 162* | 66 | AB de Villiers | S.Africa | W.Indies | Sydney | 27.2.2015 |
| 6 | 175* | 138 | Kapil Dev | India | Zimbabwe | Tunbridge Wells | 18.6.1983 |
| 7 | 89 | 67 | Darren Sammy | W.Indies | Ireland | Nelson | 16.2.2015 |
| 8 | 72* | 84 | Heath Streak | Zimbabwe | N.Zealand | Bloemfontein | 8.3.2003 |
| 9 | 64 | 83 | Andy Bichel | Australia | N.Zealand | Port Elizabeth | 11.3.2003 |
| 10 | 48* | 36 | Daren Powell | W.Indies | S.Africa | St.George's | 10.4.2007 |
| 11 | 43 | 16 | Shoaib Akhtar | Pakistan | England | Cape Town | 22.2.2003 |

# Opening pair both recording a hundred the same innings

| Openers | Scores | For | Opponent | Venue | Date |
|---------|--------|-----|----------|-------|------|
| Upul Tharanga | 133 | S.Lanka | Zimbabwe | Kandy | 10-3-2011 |
| Tillakaratne Dilshan | 144 | | | | |
| Upul Tharanga | 102* | S.Lanka | England | Colombo,RPS | 26-3-2011 |
| Tillakaratne Dilshan | 108* | | | | |

## Batsmen dismissed run-out in the nervous nineties

| Runs | Balls | SR | Batsman | For | Opponent | Venue | Date |
|---|---|---|---|---|---|---|---|
| 99 | 88 | 112.50 | Adam Gilchrist | Australia | S.Lanka | Centurion | 7.3.2003 |
| 97 | 118 | 82.20 | Martin Crowe | N.Zealand | England | The Oval | 9.6.1983 |
| 97 | 142 | 68.30 | Sourav Ganguly | India | S.Africa | Hove | 15.5.1999 |
| 97 | 79 | 122.78 | Andy Balbirnie | Ireland | Zimbabwe | Hobart | 7.3.2015 |
| 96 | 128 | 75.00 | Jacques Kallis | S.Africa | India | Hove | 15.5.1999 |
| 93 | 102 | 91.17 | Mohammad Azharuddin | India | Australia | Brisbane | 1.3.1992 |
| 93 | 105 | 88.57 | Ahmed Shehzad | Pakistan | UAE | Napier | 4.3.2015 |
| 92 | 75 | 122.66 | Michael Clarke | Australia | S.Africa | Basseterre | 24.3.2007 |
| 92 | 70 | 131.42 | AB de Villiers | S.Africa | Australia | Basseterre | 24.3.2007 |
| 91 | 83 | 109.63 | Martin Crowe | N.Zealand | Pakistan | Auckland | 21.3.1992 |
| 90 | 82 | 109.75 | Paul Collingwood | England | Ireland | Providence | 30.3.2007 |

## Batsmen dismissed hit-wicket

| Runs | Batsman | For | Opponent | Venue | Date |
|---|---|---|---|---|---|
| 7 | Roy Frederics | W.Indies | Australia | Lord's | 21-6-1975 |
| 21 | Franklyn Dennis | Canada | England | Manchester | 13-6-1979 |
| 6 | Maurice Odumbo | Kenya | W.Indies | Pune | 29-2-1996 |
| 3 | Gary Kirsten | S.Africa | W.Indies | Karachi | 11-3-1996 |
| 9 | Joe Harris | Canada | S.Lanka | Paarl | 19-2-2003 |
| 0 | Maurice Odumbo | Kenya | W.Indies | Kimberley | 4-3-2003 |
| 67 | Vusi Sibanda | Zimbabwe | Ireland | Kingston | 15-3-2007 |
| 35 | Regis Chakabva | Zimbabwe | UAE | Nelson | 19-2-2015 |
| 39 | Misbah-ul-Haq | Pakistan | Ireland | Adelaide | 15-3-2015 |

## Quickest 150

| Runs | Balls to 150 | Batsman | For | Opponent | Venue | Date |
|---|---|---|---|---|---|---|
| 162* | 64 | Abraham de Villiers | S.Africa | W.Indies | Sydney | 27-2-2015 |
| 160 | 116 | Imran Nazir | Pakistan | Zimbabwe | Kingston | 21-3-2007 |
| 178 | 116 | David Warner | Australia | Afghanistan | Perth | 4-3-2015 |
| 215 | 126 | Chris Gayle | W.Indies | Zimbabwe | Canberra | 24-2-2015 |
| 237* | 134 | Martin Guptill | N.Zealand | W.Indies | Wellington | 21-3-2015 |

The exact balls are not known in the case of Vivian Richards (181 off 125 balls)
vs Sri Lanka at Karachi on October 13, 1987

## Quickest 100

| Balls to 100 | Player | Score | Balls | For | Opponent | Venue | Date |
|---|---|---|---|---|---|---|---|
| 50 | Kevin O'Brien | 113 | 63 | Ireland | England | Bangalore | 2.3.2011 |
| 51 | Glenn Maxwell | 102 | 53 | Australia | Sri Lanka | Sydney | 8.3.2015 |
| 52 | Abraham de Villiers | 162* | 66 | South Africa | West Indies | Sydney | 27.2.2015 |
| 66 | Matthew Hayden | 101 | 68 | Australia | S.Africa | Basseterre | 24.3.2007 |
| 67 | John Davison | 111 | 76 | Canada | W.Indies | Centurion | 23.2.2003 |
| 70 | Paul Stirling | 101 | 72 | Ireland | Netherlands | Kolkata | 18.3.2011 |
| 70 | Kumar Sangakkara | 117* | 86 | Sri Lanka | England | Wellington | 1.3.2015 |
| 72 | Adam Gilchrist | 149 | 104 | Australia | S.Lanka | Bridgetown | 28.4.2007 |
| 73 | Kumar Sangakkara | 105 | 76 | Sri Lanka | Bangladesh | Melbourne | 26.2.2015 |
| 79 | Shaiman Anwar | 106 | 83 | UAE | Ireland | Brisbane | 25.2.2015 |
| 79 | Brendan Taylor | 121 | 91 | Zimbabwe | Ireland | Hobart | 7.3.2015 |
| 80 | Mahela Jayawardene | 100 | 81 | Sri Lanka | Canada | Hambantota | 20.2.2011 |

## Quicket 50

| Balls to 50 | Player | Score | Balls | For | Opponent | Venue | Date |
|---|---|---|---|---|---|---|---|
| 18 | Brendon McCullum | 77 | 25 | New Zealand | England | Wellington | 20.2.2015 |
| 20 | Brendon McCullum | 52* | 21 | New Zealand | Canada | Gros Islet | 22.3.2007 |
| 20 | Angelo Matthews | 51 | 21 | Sri Lanka | Scotland | Hobart | 11.3.2015 |
| 21 | Brendon McCullum | 50 | 24 | New Zealand | Australia | Auckland | 28.2.2015 |
| 21 | Mark Boucher | 75* | 31 | South Africa | Netherlands | Basseterre | 16.3.2007 |
| 21 | Glenn Maxwell | 88 | 39 | Australia | Afghanistan | Perth | 4.3.2015 |
| 22 | Mark Boucher | 52 | 23 | South Africa | West Indies | St.George's | 10.4.2007 |
| 22 | Dinesh Chandimal | 52* | 24 | Sri Lanka | Australia | Sydney | 8.3.2015 |
| 22 | Brendon McCullum | 59 | 26 | New Zealand | South Africa | Auckland | 24.3.2015 |
| 23 | Brian Lara | 73 | 40 | West Indies | Canada | Centurion | 23.2.2003 |
| 23 | John Davison | 52 | 31 | Canada | New Zealand | Gros Islet | 22.3.2007 |
| 23 | Kieron Pollard | 60 | 27 | W.Indies | Netherlands | Delhi | 28.2.2011 |

## A double hundred and a hundred in the same innings

| Players | For | Opponent | Venue | Date |
|---|---|---|---|---|
| Chris Gayle (215) and Marlon Samuels (133 not out) | W.Indies | Zimbabwe | Canberra | 24-2-2015 |

## Most sixes overall

| Bowler | For | M | I | 6s | 4s |
|---|---|---|---|---|---|
| Abraham de villiers | SA | 23 | 22 | 37 | 121 |
| Chris Gayle | WI | 26 | 26 | 37 | 90 |
| Ricky Ponting | Aus | 46 | 42 | 31 | 145 |
| Brendon McCullum | NZ | 34 | 27 | 29 | 77 |
| Herschelle Gibbs | SA | 25 | 23 | 28 | 106 |
| Sanath Jayasuriya | SL | 38 | 37 | 27 | 120 |
| Sachin Tendulkar | India | 45 | 44 | 27 | 241 |

# World Cup records - 1975 to 2015

RAJESH KUMAR

## Most sixes in an innings

| Batsman | For | 6s | 4s | Runs | Balls | Opponent | Venue | Date |
|---|---|---|---|---|---|---|---|---|
| Chris Gayle | WI | 16 | 10 | 215 | 147 | Zimbabwe | Canberra | 24-2-2015 |
| Martin Guptill | NZ | 11 | 24 | 237* | 163 | West Indies | Wellington | 21-3-2015 |
| David Miller | SA | 9 | 7 | 138* | 92 | Zimbabwe | Hamilton | 15-2-2015 |

## Most boundaries in an innings

| Batsman | For | 6s+4s | 6s | 4s | Runs | Opponent | Venue | Date |
|---|---|---|---|---|---|---|---|---|
| Martin Guptill | NZ | 35 | 11 | 24 | 237* | West Indies | Wellington | 21-3-2015 |
| Chris Gayle | WI | 26 | 16 | 10 | 215 | Zimbabwe | Canberra | 24-2-2015 |
| Abraham de Villiers | SA | 25 | 8 | 17 | 162* | West Indies | Sydney | 27-2-2015 |
| Sourav Ganguly | India | 24 | 7 | 17 | 183 | Sri Lanka | Taunton | 26-5-1999 |
| David Warner | Aus | 24 | 5 | 19 | 178 | Afghanistan | Perth | 4-3-2015 |

## Most sixes in a World Cup tournament

| Batsman | For | Competition | M | I | 6s | 4s |
|---|---|---|---|---|---|---|
| Chris Gayle | WI | 2014-15 | 6 | 6 | 26 | 17 |
| Abraham de Villiers | SA | 2014-15 | 8 | 7 | 21 | 43 |
| Matthew Hayden | Aus | 2006-07 | 11 | 10 | 18 | 69 |
| Brendon McCullum | NZ | 2014-15 | 9 | 9 | 17 | 44 |
| Martin Guptill | NZ | 2014-15 | 9 | 9 | 16 | 59 |
| Sourav Ganguly | India | 2002-03 | 11 | 11 | 15 | 30 |

## Centuries in the first match as Captain at the World Cup

| Runs | Balls | SR | Captain | For | Opponent | Venue | Date |
|---|---|---|---|---|---|---|---|
| 171* | 201 | 85.07 | Glenn Turner | New Zealand | East Africa | Birmingham | 7-6-1975 |
| 100* | 134 | 74.62 | Martin Crowe | New Zealand | Australia | Auckland | 22-2-1992 |
| 120 | 125 | 96.00 | Sanath Jayasuriya | Sri Lanka | New Zealand | Bloemfontein | 10-2-2003 |
| 121 | 91 | 132.96 | Brendan Taylor | Zimbabwe | Ireland | Hobart | 7-3-2015 |

## Three consecutive innings of 50-plus in the World Cup Finals

| Batsman | For | Score | Balls | SR | Opponent | Venue | Date |
|---|---|---|---|---|---|---|---|
| Adam Gilchrist | Australia | 54 | 36 | 150.00 | Pakistan | Lord's | 20-6-1999 |
| | | 57 | 48 | 118.75 | India | Johannesburg | 23-3-2003 |
| | | 149 | 104 | 143.26 | Sri Lanka | Bridgetown | 28-4-2007 |

## Highest scores by Captains in World Cup Finals

| Runs | Balls | SR | Captain | For | Opponent | Venue | Date |
|---|---|---|---|---|---|---|---|
| 140* | 121 | 115.70 | Ricky Ponting | Australia | India | Johannesburg | 23-3-2003 |
| 102 | 85 | 120.00 | Clive Lloyd | West Indies | Australia | Lord's | 21-6-1975 |
| 91* | 79 | 115.18 | Mahendra Singh Dhoni | India | Sri Lanka | Mumbai | 2-4-2011 |
| 74 | 83 | 89.15 | Mark Taylor | Australia | Sri Lanka | Lahore | 17-3-1996 |
| 74 | 72 | 102.77 | Michael Clarke | Australia | New Zealand | Melbourne | 29-3-2015 |
| 72 | 110 | 65.45 | Imran Khan | Pakistan | England | Melbourne | 25-3-1992 |
| 64 | 130 | 49.23 | Mike Brearley | England | West Indies | Lord's | 23-6-1979 |
| 62 | 93 | 66.66 | Ian Chappell | Australia | West Indies | Lord's | 21-6-1975 |

## Batsmen posting 50-plus in the semi final and the final of the same tournament

| Batsman | For | Scores | Opponent | Venue | Match status | Date |
|---|---|---|---|---|---|---|
| Mike Brearley | Eng | 53 | New Zealand | Manchester | Semi-final | 20-6-1979 |
| | | 64 | West Indies | Lord's | Final | 23-6-1979 |
| David Boon | Aus | 65 | Pakistan | Lahore | Semi-final | 4-11-1987 |
| | | 75 | England | Kolkata | Final | 8-11-1987 |
| Javed Miandad | Pak | 57* | New Zealand | Auckland | Semi-final | 21-3-1992 |
| | | 58 | England | Melbourne | Final | 25-3-1992 |
| Aravinda de Silva | SL | 66 | India | Kolkata | Semi-final | 13-3-1996 |
| | | 107* | Australia | Lahore | Final | 17-3-1996 |
| Grant Elliott | NZ | 84* | S.Africa | Auckland | Semi-final | 24-3-2015 |
| | | 83 | Australia | Melbourne | Final | 29-3-2015 |
| Steven Smith | Aus | 105 | India | Sydney | Semi-final | 26-3-2015 |
| | | 56* | New Zealand | Melbourne | Final | 29-3-2015 |

# World Cup records - 1975 to 2015
RAJESH KUMAR

## Bowling - The leading wicket-takers

| Bowler | For | Wkts. | Ave. | Best | S.R. | E.R. | 4WI | M |
|---|---|---|---|---|---|---|---|---|
| Glenn McGrath | Aus. | 71 | 18.19 | 7/15 | 27.5 | 3.96 | 2 | 39 |
| Muttiah Muralitharan | SL | 68 | 19.63 | 4/19 | 30.3 | 3.88 | 4 | 40 |
| Wasim Akram | Pak. | 55 | 23.83 | 5/28 | 35.4 | 4.04 | 3 | 38 |
| Chaminda Vaas | SL | 49 | 21.22 | 6/25 | 32.0 | 3.97 | 2 | 31 |
| Zaheer Khan | India | 44 | 20.22 | 4/42 | 27.1 | 4.47 | 1 | 23 |
| Javagal Srinath | India | 44 | 27.81 | 4/30 | 38.6 | 4.32 | 2 | 34 |

### Most wickets in wins

| Bowler | For | Wkts. | Ave. | Best | S.R. | E.R. | 4WI | M |
|---|---|---|---|---|---|---|---|---|
| Glenn McGrath | Aus | 68 | 15.73 | 7/15 | 24.6 | 3.82 | 2 | 34 |
| Muttiah Muralitharan | SL | 51 | 16.94 | 4/19 | 27.0 | 3.76 | 3 | 27 |
| Wasim Akram | Pak | 40 | 18.40 | 5/28 | 29.1 | 3.79 | 3 | 23 |
| Zaheer Khan | India | 37 | 16.21 | 4/42 | 24.1 | 4.03 | 1 | 17 |
| Chaminda Vaas | SL | 35 | 17.05 | 6/25 | 28.9 | 3.53 | 2 | 21 |
| Brad Hogg | Aus | 34 | 19.23 | 4/27 | 27.9 | 4.12 | 2 | 21 |

## Most wickets in a competition

| Bowler | For | Wkts. | Ave. | Best | S.R. | E.R. | 4WI | M | Season |
|---|---|---|---|---|---|---|---|---|---|
| Glenn McGrath | Aus. | 26 | 13.73 | 3/14 | 18.6 | 4.41 | - | 11 | 2006-07 |
| Chaminda Vaas | SL | 23 | 14.39 | 6/25 | 22.9 | 3.76 | 2 | 10 | 2002-03 |
| Muttiah Muralitharan | SL | 23 | 15.26 | 4/19 | 22.0 | 4.14 | 2 | 10 | 2006-07 |
| Shaun Tait | Aus. | 23 | 20.30 | 4/39 | 22.0 | 5.52 | 1 | 11 | 2006-07 |
| Mitchell Starc | Aus. | 22 | 10.18 | 6/28 | 17.4 | 3.50 | 2 | 8 | 2014-15 |
| Trent Boult | NZ | 22 | 16.86 | 5/27 | 23.1 | 4.36 | 2 | 9 | 2014-15 |
| Brett Lee | Aus. | 22 | 17.90 | 5/42 | 22.6 | 4.73 | 1 | 10 | 2002-03 |

## Best bowling figures in an innings

| Bowler | For | Wkts. | Opponent | Venue | Date |
|---|---|---|---|---|---|
| Glenn McGrath | Aus. | 7/15 | Namibia | Potchefstroom | 27.2.2003 |
| Andy Bichel | Aus. | 7/20 | England | Port Elizabeth | 2.3.2003 |
| Tim Southee | NZ | 7/33 | England | Wellington | 20.2.2015 |
| Winston Davis | WI | 7/51 | Australia | Leeds | 11.6.1983 |
| Gary Gilmour | Aus. | 6/14 | England | Leeds | 18.6.1975 |
| Ashish Nehra | India | 6/23 | England | Durban | 26.2.2003 |
| Shane Bond | NZ | 6/23 | Australia | Port Elizabeth | 11.3.2003 |

## Most five-wicket hauls

| Bowler | For | 5WI | Matches |
|---|---|---|---|
| Gary Gilmour | Aus. | 2 | 2 |
| Vasbert Drakes | WI | 2 | 6 |
| Asantha de Mel | SL | 2 | 9 |
| Shahid Afridi | Pak. | 2 | 27 |
| Glenn McGrath | Aus. | 2 | 39 |

### Best strike rates

| Bowler | For | S.Rate | Wkts. | Ave. | Matches |
|---|---|---|---|---|---|
| Lasith Malinga | SL | 23.8 | 43 | 21.11 | 22 |
| Zaheer Khan | India | 27.1 | 44 | 20.22 | 23 |
| Glenn McGrath | Aus. | 27.5 | 71 | 18.19 | 39 |
| Imran Khan | Pak. | 29.9 | 34 | 19.26 | 28 |
| Muttiah Muralitharan | SL | 30.3 | 68 | 19.63 | 40 |
| Jacob Oram | NZ | 30.3 | 36 | 21.33 | 23 |

## Hat-tricks

| Bowler | For | Opponent | Venue | Date |
|---|---|---|---|---|
| Chetan Sharma | India | New Zealand | Nagpur | 31.10.1987 |
| Saqlain Mushtaq | Pakistan | Zimbabwe | The Oval | 11.6.1999 |
| Chaminda Vaas | Sri Lanka | Bangladesh | Pietermaritzburg | 14.2.2003 |
| Brett Lee | Australia | Kenya | Durban | 15.3.2003 |
| Lasith Malinga | Sri Lanka | South Africa | Providence | 28.3.2007 |
| Kemar Roach | W.Indies | Netherlands | Delhi | 28.2.2011 |
| Lasith Malinga | S.Lanka | Kenya | Colombo, RPS | 1.3.2011 |
| Steven Finn | England | Australia | Melbourne | 14.2.2015 |
| Jean-Paul Duminy | S.Africa | Sri Lanka | Sydney | 18.3.2015 |

## Best figures in terms of economy rate by Captains in World Cup Finals

| Figures | ER | Captain | For | Opponent | Venue | Date |
|---|---|---|---|---|---|---|
| 11-4-21-1 | 1.90 | Kapil Dev | India | W.Indies | Lord's | 25-6-1983 |
| 12-1-38-1 | 3.16 | Clive Lloyd | West Indies | Australia | Lord's | 21-6-1975 |
| 8-1-41-1 | 5.12 | Wasim Akram | Pakistan | Australia | Lord's | 20-6-1999 |
| 7-0-38-2 | 5.42 | Allan Border | Australia | England | Kolkata | 8-11-1987 |
| 6.2-0-43-1 | 6.78 | Imran Khan | Pakistan | England | Melbourne | 25-3-1992 |

# World Cup records - 1975 to 2015

RAJESH KUMAR

## All-round records

50 runs and 4 wickets in a match

| All-rounder | For | Runs | Wkts | Opponent | Venue | Date |
|---|---|---|---|---|---|---|
| Tillakaratne Dilshan | S.Lanka | 144 | 4/4 | Zimbabwe | Pallekele | 10-3-2011 |
| Feiko Kloppenburg | Netherlands | 121 | 4/42 | Namibia | Bloemfontein | 3-3-2003 |
| Duncan Fletcher | Zimbabwe | 69* | 4/42 | Australia | Nottingham | 9-6-1983 |
| Neil Johnson | Zimbabwe | 59 | 4/42 | Kenya | Taunton | 15-5-1999 |
| Wahab Riaz | Pakistan | 54* | 4/45 | Zimbabwe | Brisbane | 1-3-2015 |
| Ian Botham | England | 53 | 4/31 | Australia | Sydney | 5-3-1992 |
| Maurice Odumbe | Kenya | 52* | 4/38 | Bangladesh | Johannesburg | 1-3-2003 |
| Yuvraj Singh | India | 50* | 5/31 | Ireland | Bangalore | 6-3-2011 |

## 300 runs and 10 wickets in a competition

| All-rounder | For | Year | M | Runs | HS | Ave. | 100 | Wkts. | Ave. | 5WI | Ct. |
|---|---|---|---|---|---|---|---|---|---|---|---|
| Neil Johnson | Zim | 1999 | 8 | 367 | 132* | 52.42 | 1 | 12 | 19.41 | 0 | 1 |
| Yuvraj Singh | Ind | 2010-11 | 9 | 362 | 113 | 90.50 | 1 | 15 | 25.13 | 1 | 3 |
| Sanath Jayasuriya | SL | 2002-03 | 10 | 321 | 120 | 40.12 | 1 | 10 | 31.50 | 0 | 5 |
| Kapil Dev | Ind | 1983 | 8 | 303 | 175* | 60.60 | 1 | 12 | 20.41 | 1 | 7 |

## 600 runs and 20 wickets overall

| All-rounder | For | Period | M | Runs | HS | Ave. | 100 | Wkts | Best | Ave. | 5WI | Ct. |
|---|---|---|---|---|---|---|---|---|---|---|---|---|
| Sanath Jayasuriya | SL | 1992-2007 | 38 | 1165 | 120 | 34.26 | 3 | 27 | 3/12 | 39.25 | 0 | 18 |
| Jacques Kallis | SA | 1996-2011 | 36 | 1148 | 128* | 45.92 | 1 | 21 | 3/26 | 43.04 | 0 | 13 |
| Steve Waugh | Aus | 1987-1999 | 33 | 978 | 120* | 48.90 | 1 | 27 | 3/36 | 30.14 | 0 | 14 |
| Yuvraj Singh | Ind | 2003-2011 | 23 | 738 | 113 | 52.71 | 1 | 20 | 5/31 | 23.10 | 1 | 4 |
| Kapil Dev | Ind | 1979-1992 | 26 | 669 | 175* | 37.16 | 1 | 28 | 5/43 | 31.85 | 1 | 12 |
| Imran Khan | Pak | 1975-1992 | 28 | 666 | 102* | 35.05 | 1 | 34 | 4/37 | 19.26 | 0 | 6 |

# Wicketkeeping records

## Most dismissals in a competition

| Wicketkeeper | For | Dis. | Ct. | St. | Dis./Inn. | Mt. | I | Competition |
|---|---|---|---|---|---|---|---|---|
| Adam Gilchrist | Aus. | 21 | 21 | 0 | 2.100 | 10 | 10 | 2002-03 |
| Kumar Sangakkara | SL | 17 | 15 | 2 | 1.700 | 10 | 10 | 2002-03 |
| Adam Gilchrist | Aus. | 17 | 12 | 5 | 1.545 | 11 | 11 | 2006-07 |

## Five dismissals or more in an innings

| Dis. | Ct. | St. | Wicketkeeper | For | Opponent | Venue | Date |
|---|---|---|---|---|---|---|---|
| 6 | 6 | - | Adam Gilchrist | Australia | Namibia | Potchefstroom | 27.2.2003 |
| 6 | 6 | - | Sarfraz Ahmed | Pakistan | S.Africa | Auckland | 7.3.2015 |
| 5 | 5 | - | Syed Kirmani | India | Zimbabwe | Leicester | 11.6.1983 |
| 5 | 4 | 1 | Jimmy Adams | W.Indies | Kenya | Pune | 29.2.1996 |
| 5 | 4 | 1 | Rashid Latif | Pakistan | N.Zealand | Lahore | 6.3.1996 |
| 5 | 4 | 1 | Nayan Mongia | India | Zimbabwe | Leicester | 19.5.1999 |
| 5 | 5 | - | Ridley Jacobs | W.Indies | N.Zealand | Southampton | 24.5.1999 |
| 5 | 5 | - | Umar Akmal | Pakistan | Zimbabwe | Brisbane | 1.3.2015 |

## Most dismissals in career

| Dis. | Ct. | St. | Mt. | I | Dis./Inn. | Wicketkeeper | For |
|---|---|---|---|---|---|---|---|
| 54 | 41 | 13 | 37 | 36 | 1.500 | Kumar Sangakkara | Sri Lanka |
| 52 | 45 | 7 | 31 | 31 | 1.677 | Adam Gilchrist | Australia |
| 32 | 27 | 5 | 20 | 20 | 1.600 | Mahendra Singh Dhoni | India |
| 32 | 30 | 2 | 34 | 25 | 1.280 | Brendon McCullum | New Zealand |

## Wicketkeepers not allowing a single bye in an innings of 375 or more

| Opponent | Opponent's score | Wicketkeeper | For | Venue | Date |
|---|---|---|---|---|---|
| India | 413/5 | Dean Minors | Bermuda | Port of Spain | 19.3.2007 |
| S.Africa | 408/5 | Denesh Ramdin | W.Indies | Sydney | 27.2.2015 |
| N.Zealand | 393/6 | Denesh Ramdin | W.Indies | Wellington | 21.3.2015 |
| Australia | 377/6 | Mark Boucher | S.Africa | Basseterre | 24.3.2007 |

## Fielding Records

**Most catches in a career**

| Ct. | Mt. | In. | Ct./In. | Fielder | For |
|-----|-----|-----|---------|---------|-----|
| 28 | 46 | 46 | 0.608 | Ricky Ponting | Australia |
| 18 | 38 | 38 | 0.473 | Sanath Jayasuriya | Sri Lanka |
| 16 | 28 | 28 | 0.571 | Chris Cairns | New Zealand |
| 16 | 35 | 34 | 0.470 | Inzamam-ul-Haq | Pakistan |
| 16 | 34 | 34 | 0.470 | Brian Lara | West Indies |
| 16 | 40 | 39 | 0.410 | Mahela Jayawardene | Sri Lanka |

**Most Catches in an innings**

| Ct. | Inns | Fielder | For | Opponent | Venue | Date |
|-----|------|---------|-----|----------|-------|------|
| 4 | 2 | Mohammad Kaif | India | Sri Lanka | Johannesburg | 10-3-2003 |
| 4 | 1 | Soumya Sarkar | Bangladesh | Scotland | Nelson | 5-3-2015 |
| 4 | 1 | Umar Akmal | Pakistan | Ireland | Adelaide | 15-3-2015 |

## The top partnerships

| Runs | Wkt. | Batsmen | For | Opponent | Venue | Date |
|------|------|---------|-----|----------|-------|------|
| 372 | 2nd | Chris Gayle (215) and Marlon Samuels (133*) | West Indies | Zimbabwe | Canberra | 24-2-2015 |
| 318 | 2nd | Sourav Ganguly (183) and Rahul Dravid (145) | India | Sri Lanka | Taunton | 26-5-1999 |
| 282 | 1st | Upul Tharanga (133) and Tillakaratne Dilshan (144) | Sri Lanka | Zimbabwe | Pallekele | 10-3-2011 |
| 260 | 2nd | David Warner (178) and Steven Smith (95) | Australia | Afghanistan | Perth | 4-3-2015 |
| 256* | 5th | David Miller (138*) and Jean-Paul Duminy (115*) | South Africa | Zimbabwe | Hamilton | 15-2-2015 |
| 247 | 2nd | Hashim Amla (159) and Faf du Plessis (109) | South Africa | Ireland | Canberra | 3-3-2015 |
| 244 | 2nd | Sachin Tendulkar (152)and Sourav Ganguly (112*) | India | Namibia | Pietermaritzburg | 23-2-2003 |
| 237* | 3rd | Rahul Dravid (104*) and Sachin Tendulkar (140*) | India | Kenya | Bristol | 23-5-1999 |
| 234* | 3rd | Ricky Ponting (140*) and Damien Martyn (88*) | Australia | India | Johannesburg | 23-3-2003 |

# Captaincy records

## Most matches as Captain

| Captain | For | Period | P | Won | Lost | Tied | NR | Winning % |
|---|---|---|---|---|---|---|---|---|
| Ricky Ponting | Aus | 2003-2011 | 29 | 26 | 2 | 0 | 1 | 92.85 |
| Stephen Fleming | NZ | 1999-2007 | 27 | 16 | 10 | 0 | 1 | 61.53 |
| Mohammad Azharuddin | India | 1992-1999 | 23 | 10 | 12 | 0 | 1 | 45.45 |
| Imran Khan | Pak | 1983-1992 | 22 | 14 | 8 | 0 | 0 | 63.63 |
| Clive Lloyd | WI | 1975-1983 | 17 | 15 | 2 | 0 | 0 | 88.23 |
| Mahendra Singh Dhoni | India | 2011-2015 | 17 | 14 | 2 | 1 | 0 | 85.29 |
| Graeme Smith | SA | 2007-2011 | 17 | 11 | 6 | 0 | 0 | 64.70 |

## World Cup winning Captains and their contributions

| Year | Team | Captain | Contribution |
|---|---|---|---|
| 1975 | West Indies | Clive Lloyd | 102 + 1/38 |
| 1979 | West Indies | Clive Lloyd | 13 |
| 1983 | India | Kapil Dev | 15 + 1/21 + 2 catches |
| 1987 | Australia | Allan Border | 31 + 2/38 |
| 1992 | Pakistan | Imran Khan | 72 + 1/43 |
| 1996 | Sri Lanka | Arjuna Ranatunga | 47 not out |
| 1999 | Australia | Steve Waugh | DNB + 2 catches |
| 2003 | Australia | Ricky Ponting | 140 not out |
| 2007 | Australia | Ricky Ponting | 37 + 1 catch |
| 2011 | India | Mahendra Singh Dhoni | 91 not out + 1 catch + 1 RO |
| 2015 | Australia | Michael Clarke | 74 + 1 catch |

## Most wins in succession by Captains

| Wins | Captain | For | Span |
|---|---|---|---|
| 24 | Ricky Ponting | Australia | 11-2-2003 to 25-2-2011 |
| 11 | Mahendra Singh Dhoni | India | 20-3-2011 to 19-3-2015 |
| 9 | Clive Lloyd | West Indies | 7-6-1975 to 23-6-1979 |
| 8 | Sourav Ganguly | India | 19-2-2003 to 20-3-2003 |
| 8 | Brendon McCullum | New Zealand | 14-2-2015 to 24-3-2015 |
| 7 | Martin Crowe | New Zealand | 22-2-1992 to 15-3-1992 |

## India at the World Cup - 1975 to 2015

### Results Summary

| Opponent | Played | Won | Lost | NR | Tied | Winning % |
|---|---|---|---|---|---|---|
| Pakistan | 6 | 6 | 0 | 0 | 0 | 100.00 |
| Zimbabwe | 9 | 8 | 1 | 0 | 0 | 88.88 |
| West Indies | 8 | 5 | 3 | 0 | 0 | 62.50 |
| Kenya | 4 | 4 | 0 | 0 | 0 | 100.00 |
| Australia | 11 | 3 | 8 | 0 | 0 | 27.27 |
| England | 7 | 3 | 3 | 0 | 1 | 50.00 |
| New Zealand | 7 | 3 | 4 | 0 | 0 | 42.85 |
| Sri Lanka | 8 | 3 | 4 | 1 | 0 | 42.85 |
| Bangladesh | 3 | 2 | 1 | 0 | 0 | 66.66 |
| South Africa | 4 | 1 | 3 | 0 | 0 | 25.00 |
| Ireland | 2 | 2 | 0 | 0 | 0 | 100.00 |
| Netherlands | 2 | 2 | 0 | 0 | 0 | 100.00 |
| Bermuda | 1 | 1 | 0 | 0 | 0 | 100.00 |
| East Africa | 1 | 1 | 0 | 0 | 0 | 100.00 |
| Namibia | 1 | 1 | 0 | 0 | 0 | 100.00 |
| UAE | 1 | 1 | 0 | 0 | 0 | 100.00 |
| Total | 75 | 46 | 27 | 1 | 1 | 62.83 |

## Australia at the World Cup - 1975 to 2015

### Results Summary

| Opponents | Played | Won | Lost | NR | Tied | Winning % |
|---|---|---|---|---|---|---|
| Zimbabwe | 9 | 8 | 1 | 0 | 0 | 88.88 |
| Sri Lanka | 9 | 7 | 1 | 0 | 1 | 87.50 |
| India | 11 | 8 | 3 | 0 | 0 | 72.72 |
| England | 7 | 5 | 2 | 0 | 0 | 71.42 |
| New Zealand | 10 | 7 | 3 | 0 | 0 | 70.00 |
| South Africa | 5 | 3 | 1 | 1 | 0 | 70.00 |
| Pakistan | 9 | 5 | 4 | 0 | 0 | 55.55 |
| West Indies | 9 | 4 | 5 | 0 | 0 | 44.44 |
| Kenya | 3 | 3 | 0 | 0 | 0 | 100.00 |
| Canada | 2 | 2 | 0 | 0 | 0 | 100.00 |
| Scotland | 3 | 3 | 0 | 0 | 0 | 100.00 |
| Bangladesh | 2 | 2 | 0 | 0 | 0 | 100.00 |
| Namibia | 1 | 1 | 0 | 0 | 0 | 100.00 |
| Netherlands | 2 | 2 | 0 | 0 | 0 | 100.00 |
| Ireland | 1 | 1 | 0 | 0 | 0 | 100.00 |
| Afghanistan | 1 | 1 | 0 | 0 | 0 | 100.00 |
| Total | 84 | 62 | 20 | 1 | 1 | 75.30 |

## South Africa at the World Cup 1992 to 2015

### Results Summary

| Opponent | Played | Won | Lost | NR | Tied | Winning % |
|---|---|---|---|---|---|---|
| India | 4 | 3 | 1 | 0 | 75.00 |
| Pakistan | 4 | 3 | 1 | 0 | 75.00 |
| Sri Lanka | 5 | 3 | 1 | 1 | 70.00 |
| Bangladesh | 3 | 2 | 1 | 0 | 66.66 |
| England | 6 | 3 | 3 | 0 | 50.00 |
| New Zealand | 7 | 2 | 5 | 0 | 28.57 |
| Australia | 5 | 1 | 3 | 1 | 30.00 |
| West Indies | 6 | 4 | 2 | 0 | 66.66 |
| Netherlands | 3 | 3 | 0 | 0 | 100.00 |
| Ireland | 3 | 3 | 0 | 0 | 100.00 |
| Kenya | 2 | 2 | 0 | 0 | 100.00 |
| Zimbabwe | 3 | 2 | 1 | 0 | 66.66 |
| Canada | 1 | 1 | 0 | 0 | 100.00 |
| Scotland | 1 | 1 | 0 | 0 | 100.00 |
| UAE | 2 | 2 | 0 | 0 | 100.00 |
| Total | 55 | 35 | 18 | 2 | 65.45 |

## New Zealand at the World Cup

### Results Summary

| Opponent | Played | Won | Lost | NR | Tied | Winning % |
|---|---|---|---|---|---|---|
| South Africa | 7 | 5 | 2 | 0 | 0 | 71.42 |
| Zimbabwe | 6 | 5 | 0 | 1 | 0 | 100.00 |
| West Indies | 7 | 4 | 3 | 0 | 0 | 57.14 |
| Kenya | 2 | 2 | 0 | 0 | 0 | 100.00 |
| Australia | 10 | 3 | 7 | 0 | 0 | 30.00 |
| England | 8 | 5 | 3 | 0 | 0 | 62.50 |
| India | 7 | 4 | 3 | 0 | 0 | 57.14 |
| Sri Lanka | 10 | 4 | 6 | 0 | 0 | 40.00 |
| Pakistan | 8 | 2 | 6 | 0 | 0 | 25.00 |
| Bangladesh | 4 | 4 | 0 | 0 | 0 | 100.00 |
| Canada | 3 | 3 | 0 | 0 | 0 | 100.00 |
| Scotland | 2 | 2 | 0 | 0 | 0 | 100.00 |
| Ireland | 1 | 1 | 0 | 0 | 0 | 100.00 |
| Netherlands | 1 | 1 | 0 | 0 | 0 | 100.00 |
| East Africa | 1 | 1 | 0 | 0 | 0 | 100.00 |
| Afghanistan | 1 | 1 | 0 | 0 | 0 | 100.00 |
| UAE | 1 | 1 | 0 | 0 | 0 | 100.00 |

# Pakistan at the World Cup

## Results Summary

| Opponent | Played | Won | Lost | NR | Tied | Winning % |
|---|---|---|---|---|---|---|
| South Africa | 4 | 1 | 3 | 0 | 0 | 25.00 |
| Zimbabwe | 6 | 5 | 0 | 1 | 0 | 100.00 |
| West Indies | 10 | 3 | 7 | 0 | 0 | 30.00 |
| Kenya | 1 | 1 | 0 | 0 | 0 | 100.00 |
| Australia | 9 | 4 | 5 | 0 | 0 | 44.44 |
| England | 9 | 4 | 4 | 1 | 0 | 50.00 |
| India | 6 | 0 | 6 | 0 | 0 | 0.00 |
| Sri Lanka | 7 | 7 | 0 | 0 | 0 | 100.00 |
| New Zealand | 8 | 6 | 2 | 0 | 0 | 75.00 |
| Bangladesh | 1 | 0 | 1 | 0 | 0 | 0.00 |
| Canada | 2 | 2 | 0 | 0 | 0 | 100.00 |
| Scotland | 1 | 1 | 0 | 0 | 0 | 100.00 |
| Ireland | 2 | 1 | 1 | 0 | 0 | 50.00 |
| Netherlands | 2 | 2 | 0 | 0 | 0 | 100.00 |
| Namibia | 1 | 1 | 0 | 0 | 0 | 100.00 |
| UAE | 2 | 2 | 0 | 0 | 0 | 100.00 |
| **Total** | 71 | 40 | 29 | 2 | 0 | 57.97 |

# West Indies at the World Cup

## Results Summary

| Opponent | Played | Won | Lost | NR | Tied | Winning % |
|---|---|---|---|---|---|---|
| Pakistan | 10 | 7 | 3 | 0 | 0 | 70.00 |
| Zimbabwe | 6 | 6 | 0 | 0 | 0 | 100.00 |
| New Zealand | 7 | 3 | 4 | 0 | 0 | 42.85 |
| Kenya | 2 | 1 | 1 | 0 | 0 | 50.00 |
| Australia | 9 | 5 | 4 | 0 | 0 | 55.55 |
| England | 6 | 1 | 5 | 0 | 0 | 16.66 |
| India | 8 | 3 | 5 | 0 | 0 | 37.50 |
| Sri Lanka | 6 | 4 | 2 | 0 | 0 | 66.66 |
| Bangladesh | 4 | 3 | 0 | 1 | 0 | 100.00 |
| South Africa | 6 | 2 | 4 | 0 | 0 | 33.33 |
| Canada | 1 | 1 | 0 | 0 | 0 | 100.00 |
| Scotland | 1 | 1 | 0 | 0 | 0 | 100.00 |
| Ireland | 3 | 2 | 1 | 0 | 0 | 66.66 |
| Netherlands | 1 | 1 | 0 | 0 | 0 | 100.00 |
| UAE | 1 | 1 | 0 | 0 | 0 | 100.00 |
| **Total** | 71 | 41 | 29 | 1 | 0 | 58.57 |

# Sri Lanka at the World Cup

## Results Summary

| Opponent | Played | Won | Lost | NR | Tied | Winning % |
|---|---|---|---|---|---|---|
| New Zealand | 10 | 6 | 4 | 0 | 0 | 60.00 |
| Kenya | 4 | 3 | 1 | 0 | 0 | 75.00 |
| Australia | 9 | 1 | 7 | 1 | 0 | 12.50 |
| England | 10 | 4 | 6 | 0 | 0 | 40.00 |
| India | 8 | 4 | 3 | 1 | 0 | 57.14 |
| Pakistan | 7 | 0 | 7 | 0 | 0 | 0.00 |
| Zimbabwe | 5 | 5 | 0 | 0 | 0 | 100.00 |
| West Indies | 6 | 2 | 4 | 0 | 0 | 33.33 |
| Bangladesh | 3 | 3 | 0 | 0 | 0 | 100.00 |
| South Africa | 5 | 1 | 3 | 0 | 1 | 30.00 |
| Canada | 2 | 2 | 0 | 0 | 0 | 100.00 |
| Scotland | 1 | 1 | 0 | 0 | 0 | 100.00 |
| Ireland | 1 | 1 | 0 | 0 | 0 | 100.00 |
| Bermuda | 1 | 1 | 0 | 0 | 0 | 100.00 |
| Afghanistan | 1 | 1 | 0 | 0 | 0 | 100.00 |
| **Total** | 73 | 35 | 35 | 2 | 1 | 50.00 |

# England at the World Cup

## Results Summary

| Opponent | Played | Won | Lost | NR | Tied | Winning % |
|---|---|---|---|---|---|---|
| West Indies | 6 | 5 | 1 | 0 | 0 | 83.33 |
| Sri Lanka | 10 | 6 | 4 | 0 | 0 | 60.00 |
| Pakistan | 9 | 4 | 4 | 1 | 0 | 50.00 |
| South Africa | 6 | 3 | 3 | 0 | 0 | 50.00 |
| Netherlands | 3 | 3 | 0 | 0 | 0 | 100.00 |
| Zimbabwe | 2 | 1 | 1 | 0 | 0 | 50.00 |
| New Zealand | 8 | 3 | 5 | 0 | 0 | 37.50 |
| Kenya | 2 | 2 | 0 | 0 | 0 | 100.00 |
| Australia | 7 | 2 | 5 | 0 | 0 | 28.57 |
| India | 7 | 3 | 3 | 0 | 1 | 50.00 |
| Bangladesh | 3 | 1 | 2 | 0 | 0 | 33.33 |
| Canada | 2 | 2 | 0 | 0 | 0 | 100.00 |
| Scotland | 1 | 1 | 0 | 0 | 0 | 100.00 |
| Ireland | 2 | 1 | 1 | 0 | 0 | 50.00 |
| UAE | 1 | 1 | 0 | 0 | 0 | 100.00 |
| Namibia | 1 | 1 | 0 | 0 | 0 | 100.00 |
| Afghanistan | 1 | 1 | 0 | 0 | 0 | 100.00 |
| East Africa | 1 | 1 | 0 | 0 | 0 | 100.00 |
| **Total** | 72 | 41 | 29 | 1 | 1 | 58.45 |

# World Cup records - 1975 to 2015

RAJESH KUMAR

## Bangladesh at the World Cup

### Results Summary

| Opponent | Played | Won | Lost | NR | Tied | Winning % |
|---|---|---|---|---|---|---|
| England | 3 | 2 | 1 | 0 | 0 | 66.66 |
| West Indies | 4 | 0 | 3 | 1 | 0 | 0.00 |
| Sri Lanka | 3 | 0 | 3 | 0 | 0 | 0.00 |
| Pakistan | 1 | 1 | 0 | 0 | 0 | 100.00 |
| Bermuda | 1 | 1 | 0 | 0 | 0 | 100.00 |
| South Africa | 3 | 1 | 2 | 0 | 0 | 33.33 |
| Netherlands | 1 | 1 | 0 | 0 | 0 | 100.00 |
| New Zealand | 4 | 0 | 4 | 0 | 0 | 0.00 |
| Kenya | 1 | 0 | 1 | 0 | 0 | 0.00 |
| Australia | 2 | 0 | 2 | 0 | 0 | 0.00 |
| India | 3 | 1 | 2 | 0 | 0 | 33.33 |
| Canada | 1 | 0 | 1 | 0 | 0 | 0.00 |
| Scotland | 2 | 2 | 0 | 0 | 0 | 100.00 |
| Ireland | 2 | 1 | 1 | 0 | 0 | 50.00 |
| Afghanistan | 1 | 1 | 0 | 0 | 0 | 100.00 |
| | | | | | | |
| Total | 32 | 11 | 20 | 1 | 0 | 35.48 |

## Afghanistan at the World Cup

### Results Summary

| Opponent | Played | Won | Lost | NR | Tied | Winning % |
|---|---|---|---|---|---|---|
| Scotland | 1 | 1 | 0 | 0 | 0 | 100.00 |
| England | 1 | 0 | 1 | 0 | 0 | 0.00 |
| Australia | 1 | 0 | 1 | 0 | 0 | 0.00 |
| Bangladesh | 1 | 0 | 1 | 0 | 0 | 0.00 |
| Sri Lanka | 1 | 0 | 1 | 0 | 0 | 0.00 |
| New Zealand | 1 | 0 | 1 | 0 | 0 | 0.00 |
| | | | | | | |
| Total | 6 | 1 | 5 | 0 | 0 | 16.66 |